T0207615

Ashes of
AL-RAWDHA

EKBAL AL-OTHAIMEEN

Order this book online at www.trafford.com
or email orders@trafford.com

Most Trafford titles are also available at major online book retailers.

Print information available on the last page.

ISBN: 978-1-4907-7324-7 (sc)
ISBN: 978-1-4907-7326-1 (hc)
ISBN: 978-1-4907-7325-4 (e)

Library of Congress Control Number: 2016907293

Trafford rev. 06/22/2016

www.trafford.com
North America & international
toll-free: 1 888 232 4444 (USA & Canada)
fax: 812 355 4082

To my son Khalid,
When he was a little boy..

DAY ONE

I WALKED ALONG THE BEACH as my eyes embraced the gulf's stretching waters and the calmness of its vast extended surface. The sunbeams were spread over the face of the water like a parasol of light. A ship swayed from afar, its sails touching the horizon, and it felt as though it was touching the sky. And between the sky and the sea, my eyesight lingered. Only moments had passed within this calmness when, suddenly, the horizon turned yellow and dust spread in surges like slaps on the face of water. So I hurried towards our house. By the time I reached its courtyard, the storm had grown intense. Waves of universal wrath pounded the shore, the sky was overturned, and I could see nothing but the cloudy images of our old *Nabk* tree, planted by my father on one side of the house. I was appalled to see the wind suddenly attacking the *Nabk* tree, trying to uproot it. I panicked and could not help myself. I started calling out to my family members and some neighbors. When they answered my call, we gathered quickly and managed to tie the tree with ropes attached to the fence of the house. And so it remained standing, stubborn in the face of wind, until a sound reached my ears like destiny.

"Ring... Ring..."

That was the phone, its ring reaching my ears. Was everything else a dream too? And as I was still in the dream, the voice of the Filipino maid, Proxy, reached me from afar. I heard her footsteps approaching my bedroom's door, and I said to myself, "This is surely a disaster, Proxy trying to wake me up."

"Ma'am, your brother, Sulaiman, is on the phone," said Proxy.

I was astonished at her foolishness, as I had warned her not to wake me up on Thursdays, so I repeated my warning to her, saying, "How many times have I told you not to wake me up on Thursdays, whatever the reason may be?"

I then went back to sleep trying to completely ignore her, but she firmly repeated, "Ma'am, your brother, Sulaiman, is on the phone, and he insists on speaking to you." Then she added "He stresses it is very important.

With a clear hint of discomfort, I screamed in her face, "I do not wish to speak to him." Then I scolded her in anger and asked her to leave my room.

I thought it was a joke by Sulaiman and said to myself, as if I wereblaming him, "What is that silly banter, O Sulaiman? I know that you are in the airport now going to Finland to catch up, in a few hours, with your wife and kids. What then is the purpose of these frustrating acts?" And in an attempt to recall sleep, I went on with my subconscious dialogue with Sulaiman, "I am also aware that, in a few hours, you will be able to enjoy the lakes and the fresh air, while I will remain the captive of hot weather and suffocating humidityhere."

Once again, I heard the footsteps of Proxy approaching the room and told myself in full irritation, "Oh my God! It's the phone again. I will kill her if she enters my room again!"

But this time, without even asking for permission, she was standing inside the room, and repeating in a flustered way, "Ma'am! There is a problem. Listen to the sounds outside." Then she continued in the same tone, as if trying to keep away the specter of a disaster, instructing me, "Get up and listen to the sound of bombs! That is what Sulaiman is saying."

I took the phone erratically from her and shouted, "Sulaiman, what is this banter?"

But he did not let me continue my sentence, interrupting me with a firm voice and a very clear tone through the phone, "I am not joking with you. The Iraqis entered Kuwait." Before I could respond, he continued in the same firmness and with a voice that made me feel as though he were confirming an unimaginable nightmare, "Come, and quickly now, to Al-Rawdah. I'm on my way to Al-Zour station."

Ekbal Al-Othaimeen

There was a pause, and then he added, "Ok. Bye."

Sleep scattered away from me. I did not believe what I'd just heard. As if in a nightmare, I quickly went to the window and opened it. The sounds of missiles and bombs reached me, coming from Al-Sha'ab district.[1] I told myself, "Oh my God! What is happening?" I felt the need for more information, so I called my friend Iman, but I found her unaware of the event. She too expressed her astonishment and disbelief of what I'd told her.

I got dressed quickly and phoned Gihan, my Egyptian doctor friend who worked in Jahra Hospital, trying to reach her before she leftthe hospital. Her voice reached me through the phone: "My dear, what woke you up on your offday?"

I answered in a quick and decisive tone, "Get dressed right now and get downstairs. I am coming now to pick you up. Quickly! Quickly!"

She replied in astonishment as she tried to understand my strange request, "Why? What is going on Ekbal?"

"There is not time, Gihan. The Iraqis have invaded the country. This is an invasion, and bombs are exploding. Are you not hearing the sounds outside? I am coming to take you now, and go to Al-Rawdah at Badriya's place."

"Ok. I am ready. I'm wearing my hospital robes. I will wait for you downstairs."

I left the house in a hurry and got in the car with Proxy. We went to where Gihan was waiting for us. When I looked at her, I felt that fear and horror had taken over her. She did not hide her amazement and astonishment when she saw me, maybe because she realized what I'd told her to be true.

On the way to Al-Rawdah, we did not notice anything strange, and we saw no signs of chaos. We only heard the sounds of bombs and explosives coming from afar.

We arrived at the house of my sister Badriya and I found her in a state of panic and horror. I tried to inquire from her husband about what was going on. Everybody was astonished. Everybody

---

[1] One of the districts of Kuwait City.

was trying to comprehend what was happening. Their ears were in a state of alertness, and their eyes were directed at the radio and the TV. Suddenly, I realized the importance of the radio, that device which I'd thought we'dgivenup after the appearance and domination of televisions in the halls of houses and in cafes. But there was the radio, this small, strange device, appearing once again to do its job over the air, through its invisible characters. It would becomeour most vital companion and source of information and hope over the course of the next seven months.

We heard the roaring sound of a nearby plane, so we all headed outside to the courtyard of the house. The helicopter looked very close, as if it were about to fall directly on our heads. Our hands were raised, waving to it, as we hoped that whoever was inside could tell us what was going on in the country. We were all yelling in order for our voices to reach its crew members. Then the helicopter landed on the courtyard of the school across the street from my sister's. As soon as it settled on the ground, the boys and men, among whomwas Walid, my nephew who had not yet reached the age of 14, hurried towards the school to know the truth of what was happening in Kuwait on the morning of that strange day (the second of August). My sister's husband was about to change his dishdasha[2] to go outside, but before he was done changing, he found that Walid had just came back.

As Walid spoke, his face was taut withsigns of despair and anxiety. "These are not Kuwaiti army. These are Iraqi soldiers. The plane is Iraqi and carrying an Iraqi emblem."

After he caught his breath, he looked at me to register his disapproval to the Iraqi soldiers' behavior and said, "Auntie, they went to the branch,[3] bought Pepsi, drank it, and did not pay!"

---

[2]   An ankle-length Arab garment with long sleeves, similar to a robe.

[3]   The branch of the consumer complex. In each district of Kuwait, there is a consumer complex named after that district. And there is a branch of that complex in each sub-district to provide the consumer needs of the population.

Ekbal Al-Othaimeen

Without thinking, I yelled at my sister's husband, as if he were the one responsible for what was happening, "Talib! Those are Iraqis, not Kuwaiti forces."

Talib stood there in astonishment and did not say a word. He remained silent without responding to my yelling. I wentto the phoneand called my friend Feryal, knowing that her husband was a politician. He was a member of the parliament, and I hopedto find an explanation from him for these strange happenings. Indeed, I told Feryal of what we had witnessed about the helicopter landing in the courtyard of Al-Rawdah School. It seemed to me that she knew about the Iraqi invasion, but her voice had a hint of surprise and some confusion when she said, "Why an airdrop in Al-Rawdah? They entered the Sheraton and occupied it. But a community school district? Why?"

I did not really know how to answer her. And I only repeated, "I don't know."

"Who should we call?" That question kept on being repeated that morning in Badriya's house. It was about the only question that was mentioned by all who were present. During that state of confusion and bewilderment, my other sister, Nawal, arrived along with her husband and children. She was crying her heart out, she and her children. She told us, through her tears, that while passing in their car by the G1 Camp,[4] they saw what they considered to be the first signs of the Iraqi occupation of Kuwait. They saw Iraqi soldiers firing at the camp in order to take over. Perhaps the more horrible sighting was seeing the Kuwaiti soldiers running away, giving up their military uniforms, throwing theminto the street for fear of arrest.

It was only normal for Nawal and her husband to be in a state of bafflement and to be intimidated by these scenes that had happened before their eyes, especially since they had beenwitnesses to the way inwhich the camp had beenbombed until it was completely destroyed. Since Nawal's family lived in Al-Andalus

---

4   Originally a subdivision of the British army for the Personnel Affair Department.

district that lies in the North of Kuwait City, they had to pass by G1 Camp on their way to Al-Rawdah District via the Fourth Circular Road.

International telecommunications were still working that day. Right after we heard Nawal's story, the phone rang. It was Nadia, my brother Sulaiman's wife, asking about him and making sure he wasok. We told her that he'dgoneto check on his colleagues in Al-Zour station and asked her to remain with her Finnish mother until she heard from us or from her husband.

The phone kept ringing endlessly. My mother was one of the callers. Astonishment did not leave her, and she seemed baffled, unbelieving of what was happening to the country. My mother, with her inclinations for Saddam, was one of the many who hadnot hid their admiration for the Guard of the Eastern Gate during the Iranian-Iraqi war, like most Sunnis in Kuwait. But in these dreadful moments, she did not stop expressing her astonishment and vexation along with her confusion-filled question as towhat the Guard of the Eastern Gate had done.

THE NEXT DAY

I DO NOT KNOW HOW we spent that night, and I do not remember how we fell asleep, or whether sleep really got the better of us. All these questions went away when I looked at the clock at exactly 4 am. The family's scene looked really strange. I felt as though we were livingin a refugee camp; I found the whole family almost all stacked up in one place. It looked as if every one of us had tried to squeeze him or herselfsomehow in the hall in a way that reflected misery. Some sat on the ground, another slept sitting on the chair, and another had fallen asleepon the couch. Some squatted by the radio, with looks of fear and astonishment that wouldnot leave them,

Of course it did not occur to any of us that our lives would never go back to what theyhad been before the second of August, 1990. None of us could have imagined, on that day, that that state would stretch and remain for months, seven in fact.

I went back to sleep, but it was a disturbed, interrupted sleep, until I woke up to loud noises coming from inside and outside. I got up and headed outside and saw young men from Al-Rawdah district carrying hammers and removing the metal plates that carried the house numbers and street names.

I was surprised by the vanity of that and asked, "Why is that?" Nawal clarified, in a way that increased the ambiguity of what was happening, by saying that the Iraqi soldiers werechasing the Kuwaiti army members, and then she increased my confusion even more by adding,"It seems that the young people were able to seize the equipment of the police station of our district."

I glanced through the window and saw two people digging a hole in the ground near our house, and noticed that they were trying to hidethe weapons that they were holding. I was more and more confused and asked myself, "Oh my God! What is happening? What disaster has befallen us?" I intended to talk to the two men, but before I could head over to them, they left the site and ranaway.

I came back towards Nawal, looking for news about what was going on. She gave me a digest of what she had heard from Saudi and Cairo Radio Stations. I took the radio, searching for an English-speaking foreign station. I noticed, before beginning the search for these stations, the eyes of the whole family looking at me, displaying anticipation, curiosity, and the hope of listening to or receiving any new piece of information or news report that could enlighten the darkness of ambiguity that had befallen us and explain what was happening around us.

The feeling of isolation and severance from the world had grown within us all. I realized, after listening to the Arab radio station and the vain talk that filled the people on it, that we could notput our trust in them at all.

I did not forget, of course, the faces surrounding me, filled with bewilderment, looking at me to translate what news I heard. I noticed that boredom and panic in the face of my Egyptian friend, Gihan. It seemed to me that confusion and ambiguity wereeating away at the soul of this woman, who was known to be kind and quiet, for living with us through the tragedy of losing safety and peace —not to mention that I felt that she thought she hadto hide her own personal tragedy, for she was faraway and totally cutoff from her family.

I left the hall to escapethe noise, choosing the room of one of my nieces. As soon as I sat on the bed, I was surrounded by everybody, especially my nieces. Everyone was persistent to know what news had been reported on the BBC, Voice of America, and Monte Carlo stations. I chose to tell the girls of what I'd heard so that they could convey the news to their mothers and fathers in the hall.

But what appalled and surprised me, as I conveyed to my nieces the statements of the former British Prime Minister Margaret Thatcher and the American President George Bush, was discovering the ignorance of the new generation of our children about all that surrounded them in the fields of politics and general knowledge. It was clear to me that they hadno idea who Bush or Thatcher were. I realized then how far our kids werefrom the world of politics, and how much they lacked in public knowledge. I discovered that they hadnot once tried to read a daily newspaper, and were not driven by curiosity to know the happenings around them.

The image started to clear bit by bit, and we became aware of the truth of what was happening. We realized, after a few days, the truth of the invasion and understood that Saddam Hussein decided to invade and conquer Kuwait, ending its role as an independent state. In time, and with the acceleration of events, the room of "Adhari," my niece, in which I stayed, turned into something similar to an operation room. There was a tacit agreement to isolate this room and surround it with a hint of sanctity, so that it could be far away from the noise of discussions and conversations that took place in the hall. The hall never stopped receiving news and reports of killings and escapes, which were a mixture of fact and fiction. Sometimes, a huge amount of rumors and sayings would get leaked to us. Some news and stories reach us of those who'd left the country in fearor to escapefrom the tyranny and practices of the Iraqi forces.

The subject of leaving Kuwait gained a special importance or maybe centralization. It occupied a great deal of the ongoing discussions between the family members. The opinions divided and diversified, and led to the division of the family into two teams. The first called for leaving the country and believed that getting out of Kuwait wasbetter to avoid any unpleasant surprises that might occur. This view was like a current that started to grow, especially after the aggravation of the feeling of loss of hope in any Arab solution that could hasten dissolving the situation. The other team believed that leaving the country would be considered treason, and called for staying. This team insisted on itsview, arguing for it with firmness, and its members declared that they wouldnot leave

Kuwait except as corpses to the Sulaibikhat Cemetery.[5] This latter team was led by the husband of my sister, Muhammad, or "Baba-Oud" as the children used to call him. He got what he wished for, as he did not leave Kuwait untillast year, to the Sulaibikhat.

---

[5] Sulaibikhat is a small area north of Kuwait City that contains the Sunni and Shi'ite cemeteries.

LIBERATION ORGANIZATION

ON THE NEXT MORNING, I started my car and headed towards Abdullah Al-Salim Suburb to see my friend Feryal and her husband, Abdullah Al-Naybari, the former member of the Kuwaiti Parliament, hoping to hear something tobring ease to my heart. As the door opened, I found the hall of the house filled with ladies talking and exchanging news. It was amazing that almost everybody was arguing and talking but nobody was listening.

Among those who were present, I found my friend Shaza, who worked with me and Feryal at the Kuwait Institute for Scientific Research. Once together, an extensive conversation took place amongst the three of us about the news of organized theft that the institute had suffered since the first days of invasion.

After those who were present exchanged news, they all began to ask about the future, aboutthe role that each of them could play at this stage, and about how we, women, could have an influential and effective role in the current events.

An extensive discussion began to answer the question, during which many ideas and initiatives were put forward. But the suggestion that gained the unanimous agreement of the group was to issuea pamphlet and distributeit tocitizens in order to organize their efforts, strengthen their resolve, and reinforce their desire for resistance.

That suggestion required us to provide a printing machine. Feryal said that she could procure this machine because she had onealready, but we still lacked a photocopying machine.

After moments of thinking, Feryal indicated that the school across the street from their house contained a photocopying machine. She asked Shaza and me to go to the school and bring the machine backso that we couldcopy the pamphlets and distributethem as discussed.

Without any thinking or hesitation, we agreed to infiltrate the school, but we discovered that to enter required having some equipment or tools to break the school gates andthe internal doors of management offices, especially since they wereall closed. Feryal supplied us immediately with equipment that would help us to break in the doors, which were a hammer, some screwdrivers, and some knives. Then we left the house to do the job.

I went with Shaza to the school across the street from Al-Naybari's house, and we circled around its walls. We noticed a group of Iraqi soldiers standing in front of the main and only gate to the school. We kept our distance, and I stopped the car to be adjacent to the wall of the other street on which the school lay. I asked Shaza to stand watch, and then I stood on top of the car in an attempt to climb the wall. The wall was too high to climb. As soon as I was able to hold its edge and see inside the school, I realized that the job would bedifficult, if not impossible, especially after I understood that it would be almost impossible to carry the photocopying machine, of whose size I wasunaware, and climb the walls with it again to the outside. That is when we decided to go back, since the job looked impossible. We returned to Feryal; the ladies were now gone from her house. We told her what had happened, and her eyes were filled with disappointment, for she had felt intense enthusiasm for the idea and believed strongly in the importance of issuing the pamphlet in that difficult time.

Shaza apologized then that she was unable to stay with us, and soonI found myself alone with Feryal in the house. We continued talking about the invasion and events, and we began to discuss our observations and impressions of what was happening. One of the things we stopped at was people's displeasure with the Palestinian position. Each of us expressed to the other her astonishment about the Palestinian position that had surprised us

all. We were supporters of the Palestinian issue, but the official Palestinian position and the actions of some Palestinians in Kuwait, who'dexpressed support for the Iraqi invasion, was a source of discontent for us. especially since there was no estrangement, but aid and support. Therefore, the position was strange, surprising, and shocking among Kuwaitis and Palestinians.

Atthe end of the discussion, we arrived at what we thought wasthe appropriate solution for this problem: that a statement beissued by the Palestinian Liberation Organization's office in Kuwait to clarify their supporting position to the Kuwaiti Issue so that the Kuwaitis did not get confused because of the irresponsible behavior of some Palestinians.

Feryal then asked me to head with herto the organization and tell them what we sawfit in order to solve the great lack-of-trust crisis that might happen among Kuwaitis towards the Palestinians due to the events. Indeed, we put on our mantles and headed to the organization in Jabiriya District. When we arrived, though, we were not able to get inside because of some security barriers that blocked entry to the place. When we asked whether any organization officials were present, the answer was no. But those who were there suggested that we go to the organization's office in Hawalli District.

We headed to Hawalli, and as soon as we arrived at the organization's office, we got off the car and went inside. There we found one official, so we introduced ourselves and starting talking with him about why we had comeand gave him our suggestion to issue that statement. We expected him to agree to our request, especially since we felt that he realized our concern and belie through the issues we addressed regarding the relations betwee the two nations. But the strange thing wasthat he seemed tota' indifferent, as if he'd heard nothing of what we'd said, and he enc the conversation promising that things weregoing to be fine.

We were confused by this conversation with that Palesti· official; or rather it increased our feeling of confusion. situation did not allow for this vague position. We really f that a position like thatcould potentially lead to an increase ir reactions by Kuwaiti citizens towards the Palestinian issue, tł

Ekbal Al-Othaimeen

that we'dgrownbelieving to be a crucial onein our lives. But here we wereseeing the symptoms of what could only lead to tearing the issue apart and loss of faith in it; while the Palestinian officials wereunaware.

We left the Palestinian official's office filled with disappointment. We felt unfairness and shock at the organization's position. "Oh my God!" I thought."How divided and torn apart have we become? What doesthe future hold for us?"

I accompanied Feryal to her house and then drove my car to Al-Rawda while the voice of the Palestinian official rang in my ear: "Things are going to be fine."

What "fine" washe talking about? He was obviously impatient with our conversation and displayed no sorrow towards the Palestinian position. "Oh my God!" I thought."I can hardly believe what is happening. Does he realize what we will face tomorrow as a result of the indifference he displayed to us? Does he understand the magnitude of the problem that awaits the relations between two nations thathave been connected by a special relation for years?" These questions and others kept echoing in my mind. But as soon as I went inside the house and told Baba-Oud of what had happened, he said, "It is good that you went out and were not arrested." The truth is, a lot of things had crossed my mind during that time, but the possibility of getting arrested hadnever been one of them.

EMBASSIES

As the days went by, asking about my brother, Sulaiman, became a pressing matter constantly on my mind. As events accelerated and aggravated, and concern increased, and despite my complete occupation with following the details of what was happening, myasking about Sulaiman did not stop. Whenever I saw a family member, I would ask them about what had become my daily obsession:

"Did Sulaiman call you today?"

However, no one could answer my simple question or reduce my anxiety. Since my phone call with him on the morning of the second of August, I had not heard from him. And since his last confusing call, we had heard nothing of him. We did not even know the reason for him not calling us.

There were a lot of citizens who had left the country since the first day of occupation. They'd all left without looking back. Some of them had left with their families, others had gonealone, leaving everything behind, and some had disappeared so swiftly and completely that we knew nothing about them.

Under these harsh and dark conditions, workers in home service were not in a better condition than us, nor wereall the foreigners who had comefrom different countries and who had been embraced by Kuwait in both its public and private sector institutions. The policy and stubbornness of Saddam Hussein had pushed everyone to the edge. After the possibility ofa peaceful resolution turned out to be impossible, a state of panic and despair developedand pushed everyone working in home service to look for their compatriots. Everyone was looking for reassurance and seeking a kind of salvation. These political developments led the members of these foreign communities residing in Kuwait to gather individually in homes looking for solutions and an escape from that fate. With the ghost of war looming, and all routes to peaceful resolution of the crisis being blocked, the servants' meetings intensified, and their calls to their embassies and consulates increased, as was the situation withmany foreign communities. Due to the rapid acceleration of events, the embassies of foreign countries decided to set dates to deport their citizens, and each embassy set locations to assemble their citizens before leaving Kuwait.

Therefore, it was not surprising when my friend, Gihan, decided to leave our house and head for Jabiriya District, which is not very far from Al-Rawdah. She wished to be in her house in order to find, with her friends and colleagues, the necessary steps to take, perhaps among which wasto call the Egyptian embassy in Kuwait and to leave the country with the others.

For the first time, I was overwhelmed by the feeling of the need for caution, of carefully measuring my steps and weighing whatever action I took, knowing that the Iraqi soldiers wereoccupying the country and were close to us, even continuously wandering through our street. It became known that luxury cars, especially some Mercedes models or SUVs, had become a target for confiscation or theft. So I carefully brought out Sulaiman's car, which was very small and which wouldnot raise suspicion, in order to drive Gihan to her house. I also brought along Proxy and her Filipino colleagues working in Badriya's house, and dropped them at my house first so that Proxy could gather her stuff and clothes. I had, on the next day, to drive Proxy and the rest of the Filipinos maids working in Badriya's house to the pre-determined location for assembly of the Filipino community members in order to be deported.

During the time when the Filipinos gathered in my house, I noticed a surge of deep grief taking over their faces, these faces that often looked void of emotion or expression. But, suddenly, in that sad moment, the moment of parting, perhaps it was a moment of cruel farewell after several years of company, all emotions that could express the magnitude and depth of human pain were magnified.

They all burst out in huge tears, with sharp voices like a volcano erupting coming from the hearts of those Filipinos. I could not help or stop myself, so I burst into tears with them. After we were done with this bout of crying, whose sounds were distributed like the instruments of a symphony, we all fell into a fit of laughter, like hysteria, the source of which was unknown to us.

After that fit, my Armenian neighbor surprised me with her visit, and after that sympathizing visit, we became friends. Gihan joined us after returning from her home, and my humble house was filled with neighbors along with friends from different nationalities. Everyone, in that crazy time, began contributing with whatever information and news they had. Others volunteered to provide political analyses that were not free of pessimism and raised nothing but tension.

It was known that the majority of residents in Jabiriya were from the Arab communities as well as foreigners. It was one of the districts dedicated for realestate investment, filled with rental apartments that wererented by expatriates, along withforeign schools. That meeting enabled me to get to know different perspectives on the rapid events that could not be seen by Kuwaitis who lived in their own residential areas and districts.

On the next morning, I took a hot shower and moved what clothes of mine I could, taking advantage of moving the belongings of Proxy, before returning to my sister's house in Al-Rawdah. I felt the need for peace of mind and to let loose some of the difficulties I had begun to face, especially after the matter of war had become real, and we had realized that it wasdrawing closer to us one day after the other, and had started to hear the sound of its drums. Perhaps I also felt the need to forget the question that occupied a large portion of my thoughts all the time, the question of my brother, Sulaiman, about whom I knew nothing at all at that time. I was really haunted by the obsession withanother question:Was he still alive?

Ekbal Al-Othaimeen

THE DECISION

I HEARD OF THE DECISION taken by my mother, she who had grown up in Az-Zubayr area,[6] as well as my sister's husband. They knew the nature of the comprehensive military regime rule, and were also aware of the disasters and scourges that had been brought by the military coups in Iraq. Perhaps they had tasted the bitterness of seeing the soldiers with their displays of cruelty and indifference, and maybe even anarchism, during and after the military coups that had been witnessed by Iraq in its modern time.

My mother had decided, with my sister Badriya, to leave Kuwait. She tried, during my phone conversation with her, to convince me of the importance and necessity of leaving, and I felt that she was more insistent on leaving. I simply refused to leave, and whenever she tried to convince me. I would respond, with some confidence and firmness, "I will not leave until I know what has becomeof my brother, Sulaiman." That answer was sufficient to stop their efforts and maybe give them some feeling of guilt. My sister Badriya seemed more panicked, terrified, and insistenton leaving.

Whenever the team opposed to the idea of leaving grew more adamant, the idea would retreat a little. However, my mother decided, with help and support from my siblings, who carried the Saudi nationality, to leave. And so, Badriya and her children and husband, Talib, joined them after they'd gotten our word that we would catch up with them whenever we knew the fate of Sulaiman,

---

[6] Az-Zubair: An Iraqi city that lies in the south of Iraq, near Basra. Its population is close to 90,000, and it is inhabited by clans and tribes of Najdi Arabic origins. But many Najdi families migrated to Saudi Arabia and Kuwait in the early 1980s because of the Iranian-Iraqi war.

or upon his return to us. Baba-Oud restated his firm and decisive position on the issue of leaving, and kept repeating to everybody, "I will not leave my house, except as a corpse to the Sulaibikhat Cemetery!"

In that anxiety-fraught atmosphere, I went to Adhari's room, the operation room, lookingfor news and reports carried by the radio stations. The number of radio devices had rapidly increased in the house, and news bulletins had become the only programs listened to by all of us.

But we became like we were in a prolonged funeral. Nobody was in the mood to listen to a song, or even any other program. In the three days that preceded the departure of my mother and siblings who'd decided to leave, I was very anxious and nervous. I noticed the presence of Sara, the daughter of my sister Nawal, and Shamsa, the daughter of my sister Badriya, sitting at the office table like two kittens, struck by panic. Each of them had put on a veil that covered her entire head. I was appalled by the scene of these two innocent girls, and could not help myself from screaming in Badriya's face, "Pay attention to your kids!" as I pointedto the veils that covered their heads.

Then I continued, warning them of the panic that was evident on the two girls' faces, "Pay attention to your kids, people! Look at what fear has done to them."

Badriya replied to me, ignoring my honest warning, "This is not the time for that, even if they put bed sheets on!" When I did not respond, she continued, instructing me, "When this problem is over, we will address that. Just focus on the news and tell us what is going on, and it will be fine."

After a few days, Badriya travelled overland to Saudi Arabia with her kids and husband, Talib, along with my mother and sisters. Accompanying them was a fourth companion: my sister Rabeah, along with her husband and kids, who carried the Saudi nationality. After that, Al-Rawdah's house became empty for us, and I spent my time in the company of my sister Nawal, her kids, and husband, Baba-Oud, until the end of the Iraqi Occupation.

Ekbal Al-Othaimeen

Bidding farewell to Badriya and my mother was hard on us, and we were taken up by an ambiguous feeling towards the future and what our fates wouldbe. We were without certainty of anything and without an answer to the question about our future: Will the family become whole again on Kuwaiti lands?

Due to my firm belief in the Palestinian issue, and being immersed in it, I felt, in these moments of parting, a sting of pain. I said to myself, "They became Kuwaitis on the outside, and we who stayed will become Kuwaitis of the inside!" What an irony! What a strange feeling! In that grief-filled moment, Nawal decided to send her teenageson, who wasseventeen years of age, with those who were departing. The maternal instinct was pushing her to save her child's life after news had reached us of Iraqi soldiers arresting young men of that age who were enthusiastic for resistance. There, we bid them farewell in our tears, and then returned to the house that was overshadowed by silence and quietude. We realized that our own lives would take a different path and that our fates were in the hands of the coming events and what the following days had in store for us, we who'd voluntarily chosen to stay in the country.

After the exhaustion of that day, filled with despair and grief, everyone went with an evident laziness to bed, without saying a word. The silent motion of each of us seemed to me some kind of implicit admission that each of us wouldface his unknown fate in his or her own way. Very early in the morning, I woke up in panic, like I was escaping certain death. Sleep had forsakenme, and I got up and left the bed, panicked and anxious. I felt certain that all who were in the house had suffered the same nightmare that I'd had in my troubled sleep. I then realized that the world surrounding us was not the same world, that Kuwait wasnot the same Kuwait that I'd known, and that life had become more ambiguous and convoluted.

I had to do something to push away thenightmare and thedistress that were suffocating me, so I headed to my sister and askedher to give me a mantle to put on my shoulders. From then on, I wore it as my training suit, and itdid not leave me all those difficult months. I accustomed myself to go out of the house every day, to walk the street until its end, where the house of my neighbor, Sheikha, lay. Before the invasion, I had known her, and we had participated together in demonstrations and Monday office discussions.

Most demonstrations in which we had participated, and discussions in which we were part of, were to support and demand the political rights of women in Kuwait, to stress the right of women to participate in elections and to run for the parliamentary elections, which wereexclusive to men, and to demand true democracy.

Sheikha had chosen to live in the house of her brother with her husband and children. Since her brother's house was the electoral headquarters of Dr. Al-Khatib,[7] their house became like a unique cell for the assembly of statesmen and exchange of news.

---

[7]   Dr. Al-Khatib: Born in 1927 in Al-Dahla area in Kuwait City. He graduated in 1952 from the American University after getting his PhD in General Medicine and Surgery. In 1952, Al-Khatib established, with George Habash, Wadie Haddad, Hany Al-Hindi and others, the Arab Nationalist Movement. Dr. Al-Khatib was a member of the Kuwait National Assembly in 1962, and was elected as a vice-president. Dr. Ahmad Al-Khatib was elected a parliament member in the years 1963 – 1971 – 1976 – 1985 – 1992 until he retired from parliamentary work in 1996.

Ekbal Al-Othaimeen

EGYPTIAN FROGMEN

I WOKE UP SUDDENLY TO the sound of the doorbell. I was surprised to see the clock pointing to eight o'clock in the morning, particularly because I hadnot madeprevious appointments with anyone! The doorbell ringing stopped, and violent knocks on the door started. My astonishment was interrupted by a well-known voice who said, "Open up, Ekbal! I am Dr. Fekry!"

I opened the door and looked at him, surprised. Exhaustion was evident on his face, his clothes were dirty, he was tired, and his hair was unkempt.

"What happened?" I asked him.

He answered, "You tell me what happened. I came from Failaka Island directly to you. I have been trapped by Iraqi soldiers for a week."

Dr. Fekry was one of the Egyptian scientists working at the Kuwait Institute for Scientific Research. He wasone of those people who are excellent and outstanding in their scientific specialty, but whodo not do any activity or know anything outside their scientific interests. He had moved to Failaka Island on a research project for the institute and had beensurprised by the Iraqi descent on the island. He and those with him had beentrapped, and there had been no news of them in the outside world. As soon as they had beenallowed to return to the city, he'dtakena car and come to my house to know the truth about what had happened in the week before he'd come to Kuwait.

While we were talking, the doorbell rang. When I opened the door, I found my close Egyptian friend Azza. Before I could introduce them to each other, Azza said quickly that she had finished arranging what was left of her home belongings in preparationfor travel. She added that she'dgoneto the Egyptian embassy and had brought me a replacement travel document as an Egyptian, to use in case the Saudi borders were closed to me and I had to exit through Iraq.

Right then, Dr. Fekry jumped out of his chair, gotready to go out, and said, "What travel document? Don't listen to her, Ekbal. You don't need to travel. Tomorrow, you'll see. The Egyptian frogmen will come and will finish them all. Excuse me now, Ekbal, I need to go home, take a shower, and make my calls. Tomorrow, in-shaa Allah (God Willing), I will come bringing news!"

However, what happened later wasthat there was absolutely no news of Dr. Fekry, and I never saw him again after that day. I came to know later that he'dfled the country two days after leaving my house. Even now, I still wonder what these Egyptian frogmen look like!

FAMILY

IN TIME, THE HOME OF one family in Kuwait became a center of gathering for several other families. This was these families' way to seek strength from each other to protect themselves, especially after car movement became difficult and unsafe.

Most of the citizens who'd decided to stay in Kuwait feared assault by the occupation forces and feared the surprises of the unknown. Daily life started to change its rhythm; most of the men preferred to stay at home in fear of being arrested. In contrast, the women carried additional burdens and did double duties; they were the ones who went to the market to buy the house needs, and sometimes they did the men's jobs and duties.

In that period, some phenomena spread; one of them was the appearance of a new type of market that the country wasn't familiar with: the wealth market. This phenomenon was accompanied by a deficiency in materials and goods. For example, Iraqi and Palestinian cigarette salesmen spread, exhibiting their wealth. Carts of vegetable salesmen came frequently to residential areas, and as soon as one of these carts reached the houses, the women would race to buy whatever vegetables wereavailable, not what they wanted like they were used to before the invasion days.

Getting petrol for cars became a problem for those who stayed in the country, especially after the decision of the Iraqi dictator to include Kuwait and make it the nineteenth governorate. This decision was followed by demanding the change of number plates that carriedthe name of Kuwait to number plates carrying the name of Iraq. Most citizens refused this decision and fought, as much as they could and in their own ways, the change of number plates. My sister Nawal refused this decision strongly and decided not to use the car. She showed readiness to go the farthest distance on foot, and she really implemented that decision without resorting to driving the car.

During this crisis, my friend and neighbor Sheika told me about an Iraqi soldier with Kurdish ancestry who was at the Al-Rawdah petrol station. She mentioned that this soldier was helping people supply their cars with petrol even if they carried Kuwaiti number plates. As soon as she told me the news, I hurried in my car to the gas station, but to my misfortune, I arrived at the station at the same time as an Iraqi officer who was checking the station. As soon as the Kurdish soldier noticed me, he came to me asking me to drive around the area until the officer and his entourage left. I followed his advice and left the station.

When I came back to the station, I saw the soldier alone. There was another soldier sitting and smoking inside the station's building, leaving his Kurdish colleague to manage the station. He filled my car with petrol, and I paid him gratefully.

In addition, in that period, the TV broadcasting stopped for around a month after the Iraqi soldiers seized control of the station building. When they decided to resume it, they did so with very modest resources. The program and news reports were not without humor and decadence, if not extreme credulousness. Sometimes, the broadcasting would start to conduct made-up interviews on air, for example, an interview with some Iraqi soldiers about how much they enjoyed fishing. The camera kept on capturing photos in a poor visit to the Kuwaiti coasts, where the fishing was taking place.

In one of these very credulous and humble interviews, the reporter headed to four soldiers who were fishing on the beach with the cord in the Kuwaiti method. When the reporter asked them what kind of fish they had caught, their answer was zubaidi fish (Pomfret Fish), which is the most famous kind of fish in Kuwait. An answer like this was enough to make any Kuwaiti person laugh, for the zubaidi fish always looks pressed from the sides, a black dot is on its head, and the edges of its fins are usually darkly colored. It is known that zubaidi fish swims in shoals or large groups near the muddy bottoms of sea shores and can only be fished using nets, not with a fishing rod, as they had shown in the live broadcasting.

With a made-up artificiality, the presenter connected his segments in a way void of any technical skill while sitting in an office that looked, from its apparent details, to be one of the offices of the Ministries Complex. The décor behind the presenter was phony. It had a library where groups of large, thick books and volumes were stacked. Due to my experience working in libraries, I was usually able to recognize and identify these books. They were simply nothing but copies of the phone book. I recognized them from their way of binding.

Among the other interviews that were broadcast back then were interviews with individuals to solicit the views of what they called "citizens." The presenter questioned those individuals witha clear artificiality that ensured that their answers included compliments and support for Saddam, or their participation in what the presenter called,"Demonstrations for supporting the president, Saddam Hussein."

One of my Palestinian friends who lived in the Hawalli area told me about what he had seen in one of these demonstrations and the way it had beenfilmed. This friend mentioned that a Jeep had beenstanding on the street and that the soldiers had distributed photos of the president tothose who were present. Then these peoplehad beenasked to repeat slogans such as "God save the president." They had also been dictated words to repeat about the Kuwaiti government, which they had described as "The Tyrant Party," according to the terminology of the dictionary of the Ba'ath Political Party, and then their opinion had beenasked regarding the reunification of the branch with the origin after the tyrant's decision to takein Kuwait.

This false atmosphere was always filmed with a single camera, so that the clear banality in creating these lies becameevident. The reporter and the cameraman accompanying him always appeared in Kuwaiti national costumes, wearing dishdasha, and each of them wore the headband and the white ghutra (head cover) on his head.

That is how we used to live daily, with this unbearably artificial and tasteless drama, which usually ended with and old black-and-white Arabic movie. Despite the outrage of what we used to see on that device, it was our only source of entertainment in those difficult and harsh times. I used to sit and watch besides Aisha and Sara, the daughters of my sister Nawal. However, Nawal flatly refused to watch TV, and used to call it, "The Iraqi Television."

Sometimes, we would find ourselves connecting with the story of the movie and following it with some fondness. Then, suddenly, while in this state of enthusiasm, the broadcasting would stop before the end of the movie, even without an explanation. When this happened, we would guess, and each of us would look the other in the eye laughing and say sarcastically, "It seems that the one in charge of broadcasting decided to go to bed, or received orders to do some other job."

THE NEW AND
THE NEW OLD

ROM OUTSIDE THE HOUSE, IN a way that seemed so close,
particularly in our street, we used to hear the sounds of
gunshots. We used to hear themcoming from the nearby Al-
Rawdah police station and its surrounding area. News started to
come to us of attacks on Iraqi soldiers by groups of Kuwaiti youths
who belonged to the resistance groups that had beenformed to fight
the Iraqi occupation forces.

The resistance in our district was not different in its methods
from the groups known in other countries that faced similar
circumstances. However, it seemed strange and unfamiliar to us.
We had lived in a near-permanent state of social and political peace
and the feeling of safety and security throughout our lives, for we
had never witnessed internal conflicts and had never seen or known
any coup attempts that could have disrupted the peace in Kuwait.
Therefore, seeing the fighting scene of the resistance was a cause for
concern that made us feel panicked and frightened, as if we were
watching a police movie or an American action movie in which we
did not know which one of the heroes would die at the end of the
movie.

There, a new life was born for us under the occupation. In
that life, one that we'd not known before, there was suffering that
constituted another part of our daily fate. However, those of us
who'd chosen to stay in the country had to adapt to the sound of
gunshots and random shells, whose source was unknown to us.

In this situation, which seemed perfectly surreal, there were
several sources of news. During that time, rumors and sayings

increased, and they were accompanied by true and real stories about the resistance and about the doings of Iraqi soldiers. The rest of the men and women volunteered to articulate and transfer these rumors and sayings in addition to conveying the stories and tales that some had witnessed. We called this free service of telling news "It is said" Radio Station.

We realized the intended effect of these news and rumors on our tired and worried selves. Despite our knowledge of the extent of disruption and exaggeration particular to this news, the situation supported the efficiency of this imaginary radio station, which depended on primitive ways of phrasing and transferring the tale, ata time when all the media that Kuwait had known before the occupation – newspapers, magazines, broadcast, and television –had becomeabsent.

Therefore, we found ourselves facing new realities that the occupation forced on us. Each one of us had to get along with the new life and choose suitable ways and methods to steer his or her daily life, day after day. With the fast, monotonous rhythm of events, people developed a special language. They kept deriving and inventing vocabulary, expressions, and new nomenclature. Maybe they revived old vocabulary, butit all looked completely strange to us.

For example, in those days, the word "as-satl" (meaning "a bucket") existed and started to make its way to our language. It no longer meant the bucket used to carry water, but it became a word to confuse our children's minds.

We also found ourselves surrounded and isolated, not just from the rest of the world, but also from the basic services we were used to such as water, electricity, and sewage. When the water was cut out, we started doing manual work that we were not used to, for example, transferring water in buckets to our homes for drinking, cooking, and bathing.

I still remember very well the astonishment of my niece, Sarah, when I found her for the first time standing puzzled in the special switch room staring at theemptybuckets placed in front of her. I had prepared a bucket of boiling water beside the water bucket in addition to another empty bucket. I found her confused, not knowing how to use the hot water for bathing, and she looked in astonishment atthe three containers without knowing what they meant. They stoodin front of her like solid masses, and her confusion made her stand still.

I immediately recalled the experience I had learned in the time I'd spent in India during my first university study, and in order to save Sarah from her astonishment, Iexplained to her how to mix cold and hot water in the empty bucket to have a bath on that hot Kuwaiti summer day.

One of the funny vocabulary words that was revived in this time was the word "feriah." In the past, it had beenused to refer to an opening in the center of the wall separating two neighboring houses, to facilitate communication between the two households without having to go out of the main door. Sometimes, the house had two feriahs, one on the right side and one on the left side, when there wereseveral neighboring houses withtrelatives.

After a month of the invasion, I came back home at noon, and I was surprised to see Nawal climbing a ladder at home and talking to our neighbor Om Ahmad Al-Majid,[8] so I greeted them. While talking to them, I discovered that Nawal and our neighbor had revived the feriah, as they called it, in a new way by agreeing to place a ladder on each side of the shared wall between the two houses and to climb it every day at specific times to talk, and sometimes to exchange plates of food with each other from behind the wall.

---

[8] Om Ahmad literally means the mother of Ahmad. "Kunya" (epithet) in Arabic refers to the name of an adult derived from his or her eldest child.

CIVIL ORGANIZATION

A FTER THE MILITARY SEIZED CONTROL of governmental and non-governmental organizations, the inevitable result was that Kuwaiti citizens, and other residents who'd remained in Kuwait, abstained from going to work, either because they fearedthe danger of going out on the streets or because they did notwant to deal with the occupation. As for those working in humanitarian jobs, such as doctors, firemen, and paramedics, as well as power and water utilities and the oil sector workers, they all went to work from the first day.

This decision was spontaneous at first, due to the awareness of these people of others' need for their work. It was later supported by all the working and organizing committees during that time, inside and abroad, especially after some fools started saying that whoever worked under the Iraqis wasa traitor.

As for those with other jobs, such as myself, we stopped going to work. For seven months, I stayed in the house, listening to news and receiving friends and family members in their surprising unannounced visits. I had to put up with this situation and endure that amount of human noise, which I had not been used to.

The visits to our house were almost non-stop. One good example was my aunt's husband: that old man who'd happened to be in Kuwait with us during the invasion, since he'd come to visit his daughter who lived in Block-1 in Al-Rawdah district. He'd found himself, throughout the events, away from his wife and kids in Riyadh. He used to entertain himself every evening by coming to visit my sister's husband and by sitting with him in the courtyard smoking his cigarettes while my sister's husband smoked his hookah along with the tea prepared every evening by Nawal.

But we were surprised by the sudden discontinuation of this daily visit by my aunt's husband and his disappearance for a few days. We later came to know that Iraqi soldiers had brought everyone who lived on that street out to the courtyard of the school across from them and burnt their houses before their eyes with Molotov firebombs. This was in retaliation foran attack by some of the area's young people who belonged to the resistance. They'd attacked Al-Rawdah Police Station and fired upon the soldiers therein.

My uncle Eissa, may God have mercy on his soul, was a small man whoheldhis cane every day and crossedthe street from Block-1 to Block-5, where our house was, heading to the mosque across the street to pray before coming to visit us and chat with us until the Ishaa' (Night) Prayer. Usually, people of the area would go to the mosque on foot and sit to talk and chat between Maghrib (Sunset) and Ishaa' Prayers.

My sister's husband used to tell me of "Abu Hammoud." He was probably the oldest of them, and he never stopped complaining about the situation. Every day he had a tale, especially since he was seen a lot talking to himself while walking to the mosque. The most recent of his tales was when he was prevented from going to the Fajr (Dawn) Prayer because of the curfew. He was very angry aboutthat due tohis extreme fear of God, as he always said.

Abu Hammoud did not comprehend being prevented from going to prayer due to the curfew. He came to the group one day, complainingand displeased as ever. So, someone asked him, "Why, Oh Abu Hammoud, are you complaining so much today?"

Abu Hammoud answered, "Oh people, do you not realize what is going to happen to us? God will punish us. Those soldiers ruling us do not know God, and God will hold us accountable for their deeds."

"Abu Hammoud! What happened? What is new?"

Abu Hammoud said, "Today, this morning, I went to pray Fajr in the mosque and found soldiers walking in front of the mosque. They asked me why I was out and whether I knew that curfew is from 5 pm to 5 am. I told them, 'Yes, I know, but I am going to pray Fajr.' Then, one of them answered me while waving his weapon, 'Go back home. Your God is still asleep!!!'"

At this, Abu Hammoud muttered, "Forgive me, O God. Forgive me, O God."

He continued, shaking his head in denunciation, displeasure, and astonishment at the soldier's response, and the crowd joined in saying, "Forgive me, O God. Forgive me, O God. Does one who fears God do something like this?"

SULAIMAN

FEAR OVERTOOK ME, AND MY body shuddered to a scream by Nawal. I jumped from my bed in panic and got up quickly, as if bit by a snake. I rushed to the hall to know what was happening, expecting a new disaster, but when I reached the hall, I found myself standing facetoface with Sulaiman. He was wearing a white uniform and had grown a heavy black beard. He was standing in the middle of the hall, and Nawal was hugging him while crying non-stop. I could not believe my eyes, and jumped as well towards him. I kept hugging and kissing him and, at the same time, blaming him for his long absence. Aisha and Nawal did not stop crying, while Baba-Oud tried to calm the situation by saying, "It's ok. Thank God for his safe return. May it bring you comfort and content."

Sulaiman sat in the middle of us, and as soon as he settled in his chair, he was bombarded by our questions from every direction. We were eager to understand what had happened to him since the first day of the occupation until his sudden return. Despite her attempts to compose herself, Nawal could not hold her tears. In order to cheat her emotions, she asked Sulaiman, "Should I bring you breakfast?"

Sulaiman answered calmly, "No, no, thanks. Just a cup of tea and an ashtray."

And before he finished his brief statement, I saw him taking out a cigarette box that carriedthe Iraqi "Sumer" sign, which I was seeing for the first time. I had heard of it before a lot, as it was mentioned in some Iraqi novels that I had read earlier. I spoke to him, asking about the reason for his absence, while repeating, "Tell us, tell us, what happened to you? What happened?"

With his usual calmness, and with a littlebit of cruel indifference, he playfully answered, "Patience, O kind one. I am about to tell you."

I saw Baba-Oud quickly putting the ashtray in front of Sulaiman, and he said to us, "Hey, you fool! Bring him tea so that he can tell his story." Sarah gotup and brought him a cup of tea, and he lit a cigarette from the Sumer box that he had put in front of him. He kept blowing strongly, as if he wereblowing worry off his heart. And after he looked at us, he startedtelling his story:

"Listen. You know" – speaking to me –"that I spent Wednesday[9] night in Al-Rawdah so that Talib could take me to the airport after Thursday evening. Then I woke up fromthe ringing of the telephone in the hall. It was my aunt Hassah saying in a panicked voice, 'Sulaiman! Get up; get up. The Iraqis have come upon us.' I tried to banter with her by saying, "This cannot be. What are you saying?"

Then he took another breath of his cigarette and said, to remind me of the morning of August 2, "Of course, I called you to tell you the news and asked you to come to us in Al-Rawdah."

He paused for a moment to remember the details of that day, and then he continued, saying that he'd looked out of the hall's windows, in unbelief of what he'd heard from my aunt, and seenthe sanitation workers rolling garbage barrels on the road and making a very loud sound, like the sound of explosions. He'd said to himself, "Perhaps my aunt Hassah was hearing a sound like this in the morning and imagined it to be explosions." However, it turned out to be that the poor woman had actually heard bombing on Al-Sha'ab palace, especially since she lived near the palace in Al-Sha'ab District.

Then he continued – we were immersed in his story – saying that Talib had woken up at this point, so Sulaiman immediately conveyed what Hassah had told him, but Talib dismissed it, saying, "Your aunt Hassah must be dreaming."

---

[9] In Arabic, the night precedes the day. So, "Thursday night" in Arabic actually means "Wednesday night" in English.

But Sulaiman ignored his comment, changed his clothes, and headed quickly to his work in the station. As usual, he took the Maghrib highway, and after passing by Camp Arifjan,[10] he noticed a heavy presence of tanks on the sides of the road. After he reached Al-Zour Power Station, he found the station's security officers standing in front of the main entrance in a state of alertness and concern caused by the news that had reached them of the Iraqi invasion of Kuwait. As soon as he entered the station, the station manager told him, "There isnews of an Iraqi invasion of Kuwait. Therefore, everyone has to stay inside the station until further notice." Sulaiman said, to calm him and, especially, to cling to the hope that he was supposed to travel to his wife and kids that night, "A summer cloud,[11] soon-to-be gone, God willing."

Sulaiman paused for a bit and took a sip of the tea and another breath of the cigarette. He then continued, indicating that news had reached them that some security officers of different establishments had been arrested, and that those who had escaped arrest were hidingin their offices. Therefore, he went to the station security officers and asked them to take off their uniforms and wear station workers' uniforms so that they could work without fear, and to ensure that they would go back to their homes without facing any problems. With the acceleration of events and news, he went with some station workers to fill the station vehicles with fuel. The station manager told them, "Fuel your cars for free. The station isoccupied by Iraqis and is now under their management."

Sulaiman glanced at us to check the effect of his story upon us, and then he continued, saying that he and all the other workers spent the night worrying in Al-Zour station. On the next morning, Iraqi soldiers came with officers and a captain to the station and asked to meet with them. Thus, Sulaiman and Attallah Al-Mateery went to the meeting. There, they were told that the Iraqishadplaced

---

[10]   Situated in the south of Kuwait. It is under the control of the U.S. Army, and it was used as a starting point for the American forces that were spread into Iraq.

[11]   Expression in Arabic that means "temporary," similar to "nine days' wonder" in English.

a special force there to protect the station from the Americans, and the captain and his officers indicated that they had only come to protect them from Americans.

Sulaiman and Attallah felt fear when they heard what the Iraqis had said, and they agreed to allowthe Iraqi special force to stay, but they asked that the force remain outside the inner gate of the station, and the Iraqi officers agreed.

But Sulaiman and his colleagues began to organize themselves after they noticed that the first thing these protection forces did was steal the station vehicles that were outside of the walls. They divided themselves into two shifting teams:a morning team that was responsible for operating and maintaining the station andan evening team responsible for fishing in order to provide food for all employees of the station, who numberedaround 120, most of whomwere Palestinians and Jordanians, withonly 20 Kuwaitis.

Therefore, it was necessary to provide supplies for these employees, at least to be on top of their duties and to manage the station and its operation, particularly since they were required to continue working without pay because of the conditions of the country.

Due to Sulaiman's passion about fishing, he decided to join the night team, which would sneak out through the area inhabited by Iraqi soldiers and that overlooked the sea in order to spend the night fishing.

Among the personal traits that constantly distinguished Sulaiman was his love for joking and humor, and the sarcasmthat he enjoyed most of the time. Even when he was serious, sarcasm would sneak into his words, as if he always wantedto conquer the critical and difficult situations in life with it. There, in the midst of all that drama, he began to tell us some anecdotes that had happened to him in the station:

"One time, it was almost 1 am, Souod Al-Dousary and I snuck out from between the wires of the fence, and we threw our fishing rods amidst the complete darkness. I suddenly felt something solid on my head, so I said to Souod, in a low voice to avoid being heard, 'Look, God bless you, at what I hit with my head.'Souod looked at my head and said, 'That is a rifle above your head.' I looked around, and the soldier said, 'Hey, what are you doing? Come with me.' He asked us to put our hands behind our backs, and we walked before him. He led us to the captain, who woke up to the soldier's voice repeating, 'Sir, these people have come to fish behind the fence.' The captain lazily got up, trying to open his eyes to look at us. As soon as he saw me, he said, 'This is Abu Nassir,[12] the electricity guy.' I answered, 'Yes, sir.'

"Our relationship with the Samarrai captain had grown strong, and we knew each other. He then sat up straight, called us over, and asked us to sit beside him, inquiring, 'What is wrong? What happened?' I answered him, 'Sir, these soldiers of yours saw us fishing in the sea and yelled at us, told us to put our hands behind our backs, and led us, like thieves, to you.' As soon as I finished my words, the captain yelled at the soldier, 'How come you caughtAbu Nassir? Don't you know him?' In a trembling and fearful voice, the soldier replied, 'Sir, I swear, it was dark.' The captain yelled at him and asked him to leave, and immediately ordered another soldier to replace him. Then he looked at us and said, 'Ok. Is there something else you want?' I said to him, 'Sir, we frequently get similar harassment like this from soldiers, whether inside or outside the station. We wish you'd give us a paper from you to facilitate our movement.' He promised to respond on the next day."

Sulaiman paused and took a sip of the tea and another breath of the cigarette, then continued:

"On the next day, a convoy of 200 trucks arrived from Baghdad, sent by the ruling party to ship the station's spare parts to Baghdad. Their leader came to us and said, 'Which parts canyou spare so that we can load themon the trucks now?' I answered him, 'Everything that is in the station now is necessary, particularly since it is nearly the only station supplying our Iraqi people, civilians, and military in Kuwait City with electricity and water. Any defect, God forbid, will cause power and water to be cut off from them.' He agreed with me and retreated. The captain came later, carrying a

---

[12] This is his Kunya, as explained earlier.

number of certificates, which he distributed to us. These documents were to guarantee non-interference with us, and they were affixed with the signature of our ruler"– he said this while laughing –"Mr. Hassan Al-Majid, may God cut short his life."

He laughed, and we with him. Then he sat up straight and asked for another cup of tea. He was about to light the last cigarette in the Sumer box. What I noticed, with a strange curiosity, was that the Sumer cigarette would sometimes get extinguished on its own, and other times, it would burn so strongly as if it was about to explode.

I asked Sulaiman to explain the secret of this weird cigarette, so he said while laughing, "Yes. When this captain gave us the certificates, he provided us with some of their cigarettes. God curse them for their cigarettes! You must re-light it every little while when it goes out, and you must look away because it may explode in your face at any moment."

TALIB'S CAR

THE MOSQUE OF BLOCK-5 IN Al-Rawdah District had an excellent location. It was situated directly opposite to our house. The house of my sister Badriya lies on the intersection of two streets and faces the mosque directly. This strategic location was a source of happiness for my father during his lifetime. Every Friday, people of the district used to head to the mosque to perform Friday Prayers. The mosque had transformed to something like a bureaucracy for the people of the district, a place to exchange news and spread information and rumors.

On a Friday at noon, Aisha came, accompanied by Sarah. They rushed, panting, towards the bathroom where I was bathing my son, Khalid. I saw them jostling at the door, each racing against the other, while panic was evident on their faces. They kept repeating their call for me, "Aunt Ekbal, help us."

Before I could ask them for clarification, a state of fear overtook me. I feared that a disaster or an awful accident had happened, and I was especially scared becauseSulaiman was at home that day, spending his semi-monthly vacation. I tried to overcome my fear, took a breath, and said, "What happened girls? Tell me."

They quickly spoke together, as if they were repeating a song at school: "Aunt Ekbal, soldiers in front of the house are telling us to give them the keys toUncle Talib's Jeep in order to take it."

I do not really know why I felt scared and angry at the same time. I said to myself, "Why do they want the SUV left by my sister's husband? In addition, it is almost broken-down because it has been parked for a long time." And, in attempt to calm my anger, I said to myself, "Did they not seize the whole country? What would it matter if they seized Uncle Talib's Jeep?"

I carried Khalid, who had nothing on but his underwear, and descended the stairs heading to the outside gate. When I arrived at the doorstep, I saw an Iraqi officer sitting behind a Jeep's wheel and talking with two soldiers standing besides Talib's car. I saw a third soldier standing in the middle of the street, awaiting his master's command. At the same time, I noticed some people of the district gathering by the mosque's doors to watch the scene of the officer and his soldiers and to follow my conversation with him.

I went up to the officer and said, "Yes, what do you want?"

He coldly answered, "We want the car keys."

I said, "The keys are not with us. This is the car of my sister's husband. He is abroad and the keys are with him."

As soon as I finished my sentence, he nodded his head to the two soldiers by the car, and they tried to open the car hood, but they could not. Then one of them went to their car and brought a metal tool, which I did not see clearly, and started to work on the car hood with it. After some considerable effort, they managed to open it.

I asked them, "Why do you want to take the car?"

The officer replied, "We will just try to start it; we will not take it."

To everyone's astonishment, Khalid, who was not over two and a half years, yelled at them, "O donkeys! Do not take Uncle Talib's car."

While the two soldiers were trying to start the car, I glanced at the top floor of the house to see if Sulaiman was there watching us from the window. Between the eyes of the people at the mosque's door and the attempts to start the car, I decided not to let the officer seize the car. I said to myself, "I will not let them take the car; they have taken enough of the country."

As these thoughts spun in my head, I heard the sound of the car's engine starting. All eyes moved to the officer to find out what he would do next. Since the two soldiers' job was done, they went to the officer's car, and the third soldier took his seat beside the officer.

The officer kept talking with his soldiers, with all eyes on him, and then he looked at me and said, "If you would please bring us water to drink."

I looked around, searching for Aisha or Sarah, but realized I was standing alone, holding Khalid in my hand, close to the door, and that everyone had gone upstairs, settling to watch from the window of the top floor. I knew I had no choice but to go to the kitchen to get the water.

Upon reaching the kitchen, I heard the horselaugh of Sulaiman as he said to me, "They fooled you! You thought they wanted water!" So I rushed to the front door and found the two soldiers driving the car of my sister's husband behind the officer's Jeep, leaving the area with their prize.

RED CRESCENT

URING THE INVASION, HOUSES IN Kuwait were no longer private places for family life; they either became locations for printing and distribution or shelters for childcare, or schools sometimes.

Among the houses that I visited in the early days of the invasion was the house of Dr. Dalal Al-Zeban. She was an active member of the Kuwaiti Red Crescent Organization. The purpose of the visit was to attend a lecture on first aid, given by an Egyptian doctor whose name I do not remember now. After the lecture, I went to the lecturing doctor and asked him, if he did not mind, to give a similar lecture on first aid to people of Al-Rawdah district. He agreed on the condition that I would drive him there and back to his home at the time that we would agree on for the lecture, since he did not have a means of transportation. I also had to drive him home that same day in order to know the location of his house.

I had to accept, but reluctantly, especially after he told me that he lived in Khaitan District, whose security conditions I did not know, particularly since it was inhabited by a large number of Arabs and other foreigners.

Honestly, I was thinking while I was driving him home of what trouble I could face in that area from Iraqi soldiers. I even started to question whether the doctor himself was trustworthy.

Once the doctor told me to stop when we had reached his home, I was relieved. I took his home phone number and promised to call to inform him of the lecture's time.

On my way back, I drove my car in a hurry to the main road, ignoring the speed limit. As soon as I arrived at Al-Rawdah, I swung by the house of my friend Shaikha Al-Farhan, told her of the lecture and the agreement I had made with the Egyptian doctor, and suggested bringing him the next day to give a lecture on first-aid to the women of the area.

I went with Shaikha to ask the imam (leader) of the mosque in Block-5 for permission to enter the mosque for this lecture tomorrow, and heagreed immediately.

We had another task, which was to pass by the houses of Al-Rawdah, knock on the doors, and invite the women of these houses to attend that lecture, which we did the next morning. After deciding on the lecture's time, I called the doctor and informed him of when it would be. I went, one hour before the appointment, to bring the doctor from Khaitan District, and accompanied him to the mosque. Women began to arrive in successive groups, and I noticed that the women's hall of the mosque had becomefull of women, girls, and children ina short while.

All the attendees were wearing that mantle, which had spontaneously become the uniform of all women in Kuwait for no reason except that it had become a means of protest on the conditions of the country. Another reason was that wearing mantles facilitated the movement of women under the blockade, for it hid the identity of the woman wearing it, in addition to hiding her bodily charms so as to avoid assault or rape.

Besides, it became a method of anonymity, camouflage, and to cover the exchange of weapons, pamphlets, and information. One of the greatestcontributions of this mantle was its ability, during the invasion, to remove the differences between the social classes in terms of clothing.

The comments of Iraqi soldiers atcheckpoints was often a source of laughter, due to the big difference between the photos of women when displaying their IDs and their actual faces without any decoration or makeup, in addition to being covered in black.

However, in reality, inviting women to train in first aid was not the only reason behind our personal communication with women in the area. There were other reasons. With the arrival of news about the possibility of an approaching third world war aimed atliberating Kuwait, rumors and news began to spread regarding the quantities, volumes, and technologies of modern weaponry that would be used to expel the tyrant Saddam from Kuwait.

The spreading of this news had caused many citizens to have severe psychological disorders as a result of fear. The mere idea of having this huge military buildup was enough to instill panic in any of us.

With the approach of the battle, shelters became an important demand for people, particularly because Kuwait used to lack these shelters in the residential areas. Thus, I thought I would do some stock checking of the houses in Al-Rawdah to learn the number of vaults available in Kuwaiti families' houses and to inform people of the nearby vaults to which they couldsecure themselvesat the time of war.

I went to the house of my friend Shaikha and took a pen and a paper that I hid under mymantle. I asked her to help me locate the houses where there werevaults and then record the number and locations of these houses in a pamphlet to be distributed later on topeople in case of war.

Indeed, we started our tour, and wewent knocking on the doors to locate the vaults of houses and write down the number of houses that containedthe vaults. When the job was done, we went to Shaikha's house, and she copied the list for herself as well, in order to help distribute towomen of the area.

The strange and amazing thing was when the airstrike began and the war broke out, we actually stayed in my sister's house in Al-Rawdah, which did not contain a vault. All we did was occupy the spot below the stairs and stack ourselves there throughout the airstrike days.

THE ORPHANAGE

HAYFAA' AL-NAKKAS AND HER COLLEAGUES played an excellent role in looking after care homes in Sulaibikhat area. In my opinion, that role was really a heroic one; especially since care homes lie in Sulaibikhat, to the north of Kuwait, around Dawwar Al-Izam (Bones' Square), which was called that because the orthopedics hospital also lies on that square. It was later called "Saddam's Square" after the Iraqi soldiers placed a statue of the entombed president, Saddam Hussein, in the middle of the square.

Due to its prominent location, that square is the first thing meeting someone who is coming from the north towards Kuwait City. The funny irony is that even after it was called "Saddam's Square," the soldiers began calling it "Dawwar Om Al-Izam" (Osteo Square) as a term for understanding between them and the Kuwaitis due to the vitality and importance of the square; it became the meeting place for busses going from Kuwait to Iraq, and vice versa. The care homes were situated behind G-One military camp, where forces of the National Guard and Kuwaiti Armed Forces were positioned, and which had witnessed fierce resistance since the first morning of the Iraqi attack.

Due to these military incidents of mutual shooting, bombings, and explosions, the nearby buildings had sustained damages, and this put the residents of care homes in a state of terror, especially the elderly and the orphans.

Since the first day, particularly after the majority of the care homes' staffs stopped working, many citizens rushed tovoluntarily work in these homes, and people started donating and providing aid, material and otherwise, to alleviate the impact of the crisis on them. I want to make a special mention of the important role played by Mr. Adnan Al-Gai'an and Ms. Zainab Al-Harbi, whospared no effort in service of the orphanages' children, asking about them and providing aid to them, after Kuwaiti families embraced them.

I had my share of embracing some of those children, and I cannot forget the visits of Adnan Al-Gai'an to me throughout the invasion to ask about them and ensure I was providing them with winter and summer clothes and other primary supplies such as milk, diapers, etc.

His last visit to me was unforgettable. I saw him coming and carrying a large group of huge bags, so I asked him, "Adnan, by God, what are these bags you are carrying?"

Adnan answered with a smile that he tried to hide, "Pampers" (diapers for children).

I was surprised by his reply. "Why this size? I am sponsoring children, not the elderly."

He answered with asmile that he could no longer hide, "Dear, our supplyof diapers had run out, so we had to buy kids' diapers from Iraq. These are made in Iraq."

On the next day, I made the kids wear these "Pampers" and tried to attach the adhesive tape, but whenever one of them stood up, the tape would become unattached and the diaper would fall on the ground, spread out like a white towel.

Then I thought of putting the diaper on the childandsupporting it with one or more pairs of underpants, to hold it on and avoid its dropping.

I was convinced of that solution, which seemed practical to me. One day, I went out of the house in the early morning to run some errands, and when I returned, I discovered that I had not given the children their daily bath. I looked at them, and I found them all wearing the diapers and undershirts only. I was surprised atthe diapers resilience, despite the fact that the kids were playing all the time and were without any underpants for supports. I called one of the girls to change her diaper and found out that Sarah, my niece, had already bathed them and changed their diapers, and that she had attached each diaper with adhesive tape of the type used with paper, and she'd made it so tight that I found it difficult to un-attach it without using scissors.

Upon the approach of the airstrike, after its announcement, we were told that those responsible for orphanages would vacate them all and distribute the residents tovolunteering families who would care for the orphansin that difficult period, which we knew not how it would turn out.

I went with Shaikha Al-Farhan to a care home and brought along two children. After we did the registration, we noticed a beautiful young girl among them; she looked somehow special, as if she werereceiving special care. Shaikha expressed her desire to take that girl also, but her request was denied. Shaikha was displeased at the denial ofher request to take the girl, which was for reasons that they refused to disclose.

AL-QADSIYA

I FELT INSOMNIA. I COULD NOT sleep most of the days, but I sometimes slept very deeply. This day, I woke up early to the phone ringing. I felt that the phone had become an obsession in my life. I listened as someone picked up the phone, and then I heard the voice of Nawal, who spoke for a little while with the caller and then hung up.

I then heard Nawal tell her husband, Muhammad, "Your sister, Lulua, says that your mother is sick and would like to see you."

Muhammad replied, "May God speed her recovery."

He paused for a while, as if reconsidering, and then said, "I will call her later."

I entered the hall, and Nawal told me, "Would you go with me today to Al-Qadsiya complex to buy some stuff and then go visit Aunt Fatima? Lulua says she is sick."

I nodded my head in agreement.

Al-Qadsiya District is only separated from Al-Rawdah District by one bridge. We crossed the bridge and went to Aunt Fatima's house first. Lulua welcomed us, and we greeted our aunt. She asked us about her son, Muhammad, and told us not to let him go out to the street in order not to let the Iraqi soldiers arrest him. We reassured her that Nawal and I were the ones who went out for shopping and other errands, so she was satisfied.

Lulua accompanied us to the other hall to continue organizing it. There, I saw that the mattresses were aligned around the hall and the couches had been removed from their place and used to block the hall's door that overlooked the outer courtyard. I asked her, "Who sleeps here, if you sleep in the other hall?"

She answered in a low voice, hesitantly, "Abdullah" – her brother –"and his friends come at noon for lunch, and in the evening to sleep. In the morning, they go to Abdullah's house, and I do not know where they go afterwards!!" She paused for a moment and then continued, "Poor them. Did you see the covers that glow at night when the lights are out?! I had bought them before the invasion for my kids, and on the first night when Abdullah and his friends came to sleep, we turned the lights out. I brought the new covers, and after one minute, these covers began displaying phosphoric colors, so they yelled at me to change them, since the glow of these covers couldbe seen through the window from the outside."

We laughed, and her eyes went teary, and she said, "God save them. By God, I fear for Abdullah."

We knew then that Abdullah had some activity in the resistance, and it was evident that Lulua did not wish to provide more information, and so we did not ask her about the nature of his activities.

Nawal said, "God is the Protector."

We heard the door ringing, and Lulua expressed her surprise that someone was knocking, for she was not expecting anyone. I understood her concern, since she was afraid of soldiers raiding her house, especially since her husband was a colonel in the army and was abroad during the invasion.

But when she opened the door, she found a familiar face, Om Abdullah, her neighbor and friend, who entered while shivering from fear. Luluabrought her a glass of cold water while she anxiously asked her about what happened.

Lulua asked,"What is with you? Did they take Abu Abdullah? Has something happened to your kids?"

Om Abdullah replied,"No, no... Do not worry, nothing happened to us... But God curse Kantoa, our Ceylonese maid. She stole all our gold!"

Here, we all yelled,"What?!"

Om Abdullah answered,"Did we not hear that, in Sabah Al-Salim District, they searched the houses and even tore pillows apart? So my sisters-in-law and I removed all our gold from the pillows and dug a hole in the house, put our gold in it, and covered it with ceramic. After we were done, one of my sisters-in-law called Kantoa and asked her to clean the dust. After a few days, Kantoa asked to leave us. We were surprised since, at the beginning of the invasion, she'd told us she did not wish to go to Ceylon. Anyway, a few days after she left, Abu Abdullah asked me to go and check out the gold, and we went nuts, my sisters-in-law and I, when we discovered that the gold, jewelry, and watches weregone. I went yesterday to her sister's house, and I found her there and asked her to bring the jewelry. I threatened her that if she did not bring back the gold, I would take her to the police station. When I found no response on her part, I took her angrily to Al-Qadsiya Police Station."

Lulua asked,"Did you really go to the police station voluntarily?"

Om Abdullah replied,"I was angry. All my gold and my girls' gold! By God, I was not afraid of the soldiers."

Then she added that when she entered the officer's room, she was shocked to see around six sleeping beds on which sata group of soldiers with their full weapons.

Om Abdullah continued with her story:

Fear went into me, so I gave him my ID. Then the officer asked,"What is with you?"

I told him that the maid had stolen my gold.

He said, "What a fool! Where did you put your gold? And why do you have a maid? Are you disabled? Don't you have hands to work with?"

I did not expect his answer or his offensiveness, so I answered, "I have a disabled son who needs help."

He answered, "And where was your gold?"

"I dug a hole in the house and buried it therein."

"Why would one put this gold in a hole, you fool?"

Fearfully trying to cover my lie, I said,"There are Palestinian gangs that steal things, and I feared for the gold."

"Palestinian gangs, huh. Where is your man?"

"My man is sick with a heart disease."

"This terrible doing of yours will give him a heart attack. Tell me, how much is this gold of yours?"

I told him, "Eight thousand Kuwaiti dinar."

Here, the officer turned to the soldier beside him and said, "Write it as Iraqi dinar." Then he turned back to me and asked, "Why do you have this amount of gold? Do you run a jewelry shop?"

I fearfully said, "No, this is not just my gold; this is the gold of all the women and girls of the family."

Then he asked one of his soldiers to go to the house to inspect the location of the hole and to find the address of the maid's family in Kuwait.

This morning, they called me and asked me to go to the police station. I went, and they told me that they had found the maid and interrogated her but did not find anything with her! God curse them! They must have beaten her until she guided them to the gold, and they took it.

We tried to calm her down, unsuccessfully. Then Lulua took leave to prepare lunch, saying, "I have to arrange the house and prepare lunch for Abdullah and his group."

With that, we left and bidthem farewell.

After liberation, I knew what Lulua had hidden from us regarding "Abdullah's group." They were with Sheikh Sabah Al-Nassir, the former Undersecretary of the Ministry of Defense, the one responsible for organizing the resistance media and political coverage in the country during the Iraqi invasion and the leader of "Bu Nasir Group," as well as with some of the other group members.

SOLDIERS IN OUR HOUSE

ONE DAY IN OCTOBER, WE were surprised by some of the Iraqi soldiers, who broke the entrance door of the hall facing the outer door of the house. They had come to search the house, and they knocked on the door with their fists. And since we did not hear these knocks, they broke down the door. The hall in the ground floor faced the main door's entrance, before one of these meetings.

Therefore, that door became open all the time, and it was no longer possible to close it. In order to avoid the soldiers' harassment, we decided to place a solid metal table behind the glass door of the hall. That way, the hall was tightly closed, and entrance to the hall was only possible via the windows that extended down to the hall's floor. Whoever wanted to enter the house had to bow down a little to be able to enter through the window, which became the sole entrance to the house. As for the outer door, it remained unlocked, as was the usual case before the invasion.

One evening, Sarah and Aisha saw some Iraqi soldiers entering our house and thendecidingto sit by the pool. They extended their legs and started talking and conversing, unaware that we lived in the house. They were a group of soldiers who stayed in the school across the street. When I heard what Sarah and Aisha recounted, I did not believe their story at first. However, I noticed panic on Nawal's face, and she started telling her husband to do something, urging him to close the glass windows. She had grown extremely scared and anxious after hearing stories of Iraqi soldiers raping women and girls, and she said to her husband, "I have girls, and soldiers might raid the house to rape them."

I noticed hints of despair and fear covering Baba-Oud's face, for he had not forgotten the beating he'd gottenfromthe soldiers on one of their visits to our house. Since then, he'd never left the house except once, when he'dgoneto bury his aunt in Sulaibikhat Cemetery.

After that conversation between Nawal and her husband, I headed for the swimming pool, and I was shocked to see the footprints of soldiers all over the place. I asked my sister to put her mantle on and follow me to the car. We headed towards the Shuwaikh Industrial Area and went through its streets, whichlooked abandoned and void but forsome Arab workers and some Iraqi soldiers with no idea of the reason for their presence in that forsaken area. Most of the shops were closed, which made us worry even more. As we drove around the area, we found a metal workshop, so I stopped the car and headed inside. I found the owner, a blacksmith of Palestinian origin, and despite my composure and pretendedcoolness, fear overtook me. While talking to him, I found myself– I, who wasobsessed with and enthusiastic for the Palestinian cause – feeling injustice and lack of confidence in the Palestinians, since the majority of them semi-blindly and absolutely sided with the tyrant of Iraq and approved of occupying and taking Kuwait in.

After I explained my request to the blacksmith, he agreed to place a metal grid on the outer and inner doors of the hall, and other metal grids on its windows. After we agreed on the price and fare, he told me that he needed to take the measurements of the doors and windows, and indicated that he did not have a car. We were not surprised by his request to come to our house, to take the measurements, as long as we returned him again to Shuwaikh Industrial Area. Since we had need ofhim, we reluctantly and fearfully agreed.

The car was small, so he sat in the back seat. But as soon as he sat there, I was haunted by many thoughts, implications, and questions. I said to myself, "Does he have a gun? Will he force us, on the way back, to stop in front of a station for Iraqi soldiers?" And there, dark thoughts and nightmares kept rushing through my imagination, and perhaps Nawal's imagination as well. Despite that dark feeling brewing in my heart, I composed myself and drove the car towards the house. However, I could not overcome the thought of assault on me or Nawal throughout the drive. I fully expected that, at one moment or the other, he would suddenly extend his hand to my throat or hers to strangle us, or to do something to harm us. As soon as the residential area houses appeared to us, we breathed a sigh of relief and felt some kind of comfort, which we expressed by the smiles that appeared on our faces after a long period of glooming.

At home, we agreed with him to place grids of metal rods similar to those that surround prisons. After two days, he installed these grids on the doors and windows, which seemed to us like metal rods for an ancient prison.

TUESDAY GATHERINGS

IN THESE STRANGE TIMES, I continued to invite friends and work colleagues to my house every other week. That semi-monthly assembly became a kind of consolation for us to resist boredom, tedium, fear, and anxiety. Most of these gatherings would coincide with the arrival of my brother Sulaiman from Al-Zour for his semi-monthly vacation. His arrival every time was enough to organize a party to celebrate him after an absence that was a source of daily anxiety for me.

My sister Nawal had decided to store whatever meat and vegetables she found in the market in the fridge throughout the two weeks preceding Sulaiman's arrival. His arrival was a source of great joy for us, and Nawal would prepare a luxurious and deluxe meal, at least by the standards of those days. I noticed the energy that would flow into Sarah and Aisha from their happiness to meet my friends and for the presence of their uncle, Sulaiman. He never stopped telling the stories and adventures of him and his friends with the Iraqi soldiers. He looked like the knight of his time as he told us, in his usual gentleness and sense of humor, the stories that happened with the Iraqi army in Al-Zour station.

These visits became a special ceremony. At first, there was no set time for their ending or even beginning. Some friends came accompanied by their husbands, who had driven them to the house. The husband would usually squeeze in a number of kids in his car to act as a shield or a way to avoid problems that the Iraqi soldiers might cause on his way back after driving his wife. Some friends chose to walk to the house in the evening, and others chose means suitable to the conditions.

Tuesday had become the appointment of meeting loved ones and friends, in the presence of Sulaiman mostly, butwithout him sometimes.

In one of these gatherings, in which he was present with a number of my friends, we exchanged news, rumors, sayings, and the happenings of the country, as usual. Sometimes, the discussion would grow intense; everyone would present his analysis of the overall Arabian situation and the condition of the country according to the logic he or she viewed as valid. We would frequently differ in opinions and views. However, we would all, whether Kuwaitis or Arabs, agree on a pivotal and fundamental issue: the return of Kuwait and the end of the occupation. Every one of these Tuesday gatherings would end, one way or another, with this agreement that included stressing on that belief.

However, there was one time when my belief was shaken so much that my certainty of the return of Kuwait weakened. It happened when I met a friend of a Palestinian origin. He was working with me in the Kuwait Institute for Scientific Research, and he wasa physicist. He had returned to Kuwait in order to move his stuff and car to Jordan. The most distinct feature of that friend was his deep pessimism regarding many issues that concerned public affairs and politics; he would sometimes be extreme in his pessimism. The day that I met him, I was struck by real panic. He kept reassuring me that the Kuwaiti cause wasfinished, and he supported his view with much alleged evidence, including the declining interest in the news related to the Kuwaiti cause in the global media and that terrifying fact that the occupation no longer had priority on all the Arab and foreign news stations.

Not only that, but he also kept pressuring me to think and make an immediate decision, clarifying that I had to choose between being a Kuwaiti of the inside or a Kuwaiti of the outside. He kept increasing my pain through his imaginary exaggerations as he said, "If you leave Kuwait, you will never be able to see it again, just like what happened with the Palestinians who chose to leave Palestine."

Ekbal Al-Othaimeen

That night, all the anxiety of the world overcame me, and I could not sleep. The echoes of his words kept ringing in my ears, and I never stopped thinking about making the decision to stay, and the inevitability of perseverance, whatever the outcome of that decision was. Visions and imaginations kept engaging my mind, and before me, I began to see the outcome scenes of my decision. Situations kept successively summoning one another before my eyes, so I rolled over and cried.

Eventually, however, Tuesday assembly was not void of humor, frivolity, and banter. I remember, for example, that one of my friends, and she was a Kuwaiti who'd lived all of her life abroad in Lebanon and France, had lacked the intimate knowledge of the situation in Kuwait and the Arab region, and she spoke in a Lebanese accent.

It was bad luck that she chose to return to Kuwait after getting her PhD – shortly before the Iraqi invasion. She was a Tuesday assembly regular, so she would listen to our analyses with some astonishment, but she would surprise us every now and then with a strange and funny suggestion that would make us laugh.

For example, she once suggested that the crisis could be resolved if Kuwait pressured Sri Lanka and demanded they stop exporting tea to Iraq and Kuwait. Then she innocently continued, "If the exportation of tea stopped, the Iraqi soldiers would die, because they cannot bear living without it." And she enthusiastically concluded, "If the Kuwaiti government adopted this solution, they would save us from this calamity."

I cannot also forget "Shoush," my Armenian friend, who kept a copy of the book *Prophecies of Nostradamus*; it would never leave her bag. She was keen on reading, and she never stopped blaming us by saying, "Had you been a reading nation, you would have made use of the prophecies of Nostradamus regarding the invasion of Kuwait." Then she would take her copy of the prophecies book and start reading, explaining, and interpreting that prophecy. She would stop at the English term "Mabus" and clarify that if that word was reversed, we would get the name of the tyrant Saddam. Then she would pause for a moment, to notice the effect of her interesting discovery on us, and then continue to tell us of the second prophecy. She would read, "The Iraqis will attack Spain. People will either take themselves, be laughing, go eating, or be asleep. The pope will escape to an area near the Rhône; Italy and the Vatican will be occupied." And without giving us a chance to ponder, she would say while showing the pride of the victorious, "The prophecy here describes the invasion of Kuwait, and that it would begin at night. People then would either be asleep, playing, or chatting."

She would proceed to explain what else was in the book of prophecies, saying that Nostradamusdescribed the Kuwaitis as "alleys of Spain," because America was discovered by the Spanish, and was a Spanish colony, and that Jews and Christians used to call prophets and clergymen "kings." However, Nostradamus reversed the name and called the Prince of Kuwait the "Pope." Then she would add, "The occupation of Italy and the Vatican means the occupation by the western and U.S. forces of Saudi Arabia, since Italy resembles Saudi Arabia in that it contains the Vatican, while Saudi Arabia contains the Kaa'ba" – the Holy Mosque –"which is sacred for the Muslims."

Our other friend, Mona, never ceased to surprise and amaze the audience. As soon as the discussion ended, she would ask her strange question that was repeated a lot, "Don't you think that Saddam resembles suchandsuch?" Then we would ask who that such and such was, knowing that she meant her boss at the ministry.

On one of the Tuesday gatherings, one of our Palestinian colleagues who worked with us in the same institute happened to be present. He was against the invasion of Kuwait and sympathizedwith us. In addition to being a member in the Democratic Front for the Liberation of Palestine, he frequently criticized the position of the Palestinian Liberation Organization on the invasion. During that assembly, he told us about an Iraqi friend of his who was an officer in the Iraqi army. As he spoke, he mentioned that he'd hosted that friend in his house. As soon as he was finished, the signs of disapproval and indignation appeared on everybody's face. The reaction of my friend Iman to hosting the Iraqi officer was very intense; she angrily spoke to our Palestinian colleague, saying, "How could you banquet someone who entered the country by force, even if he was merely following orders?"

In reality, dealing with Palestinians throughout the invasion often caused me awkwardness, especially since I was known for my numerous and diverse friends of Palestinians belonging to different political movements.

I never hesitated in providing aid to any of them, whether by organizing fairs regarding the Palestinian cause sometimes, participating in fundraising campaigns for their organizations, etc. Two weeks after the invasion, an incident happened with some of them that caused me a lot of anger and disapproval. I had goneout wearing the mantle, as usual, and gone to Jabiriya complex to purchase some stuff. Whilethere, I saw some Palestinian women who stood close to me. When they saw me wearing the mantle, they kept making fun of it and laughing at mystate; none of them spoke to me.

I remained silent and did not respond to their mockery, perhaps in fear of the Iraqi soldiers whowere spread close to us. However, I was very much distressed by their position and kept asking myself, "What reason would they have to holdthis position? Why did they unveil the feelings of gloating and satisfaction like this?"

Even now, and despite the falling of all these years, that incident still seems strange and confusing. Despite having tried as much as possible to comprehend some of these incidents, they are still mysterious and confusing for me.

But I can say that my Palestinian friend Salah Hezayien, the journalist forAl-Arabi Magazine who died almost four years ago in the Jordanian capital city of Amman after struggling with his terminal disease, was the one who was able, with his character, nobility, and deep friendship with us, to help me overcome my distress and the deep trust crisis towards Palestinians that I had. He was the one who interceded for them so that I could forget the slips of the Palestinians, both as an organization and as a nation. He was, may God have mercy on his soul, very loyal and visited us regularly, and he also helped us send mail and recorded tapes to my sister who lived in Muscat, the capital of Oman. He was always in contact with her and her family, and if not for him, our news would have been cut off from our families abroad.

Indeed, Salah played a role in alleviating the anger of the Kuwaitis at the despicable and vandalistic role played by the Arab Liberation Front, the Palestinian wing of the Iraqi Ba'ath Party, whose fighters received intensive training courses by the Iraqi army. During the outburst of anger at the Arab Liberation Front's role and the Palestinian demonstrations supporting the occupation all over the world, Salah brought to us a statement of the Palestine Communist Party in which it denounced the occupation. We, in turn, published it in the resistance newspapers at that time.

The anger of my sister towards the Palestinians was only alleviated by the repeated visits of Salah Hezayien to us, and his continuous reassurancestoher about her children and family in Muscat. Whenever a surge of anger struck her when she recalled the position of some Palestinians during the invasion, and when she started to generalize that on all Palestinians, I would quickly remind her of our friend Salah, and immediately she would mutter back, "Salah is different."

FRIENDS

MONG THE CHARACTERS THAT USED to frequent our house in Al-Rawdah was the Iraqi friend "Abu Barrak," a towering, tall friend, like a Basranian palm tree, with a child's face that expressed alienation and grief. I always saw him pulling himself on as a wounded, heavy-hearted person, haunted by his eternal obsession that always accompanied him to return one day to Iraq, which he did not.

My relationship with "Abu Barrak" as well as other Iraqi friends, both who lived inside and outside Kuwait, affected me and broadened my awareness of the Iraqi situation, particularly when I realized that most of my Iraqi friends were coincidentally of the generation that had left Iraq by the end of 1978. This was due to the large immigration of Iraqi intellectuals, the result of the collapse of the alliance between the Ba'ath Party and the Communist Party, which made the democratic Iraqi intellectual an outlaw due to his/her left-wing affiliations.

Therefore, many of these intellectuals and competencies migrated to neighboring countries to escape the tyranny of the regime. Some of them settled there, and others went on either to the USA or to another western country.

The truth is that this Ba'athist regime was not only represented by Saddam Hussein, for the crimes committed by the Ba'athist institution, of murder, rape, execution, and dislodgment had also coincided with the reign of Ahmed Hassan Al-Bakr (1968–1979). Even earlier, in the beginning of the party's foundation, its activities were linked to coups, intelligence works, murder, and conspiracy.

One of the manifestations of the suffering experienced by Iraqi immigrants, taken as a precaution against any acts of the

Iraqi regime's people and out of fear of the tyranny of the Ba'athist regime and the intelligence activities of the Iraqi embassies across the world, was being forced to assume aliases for others to call them with and insisting on keeping their identities hidden and secret.

Abu Barrak (Abd Al-MuhsinBarrak Ba-Hussain), my beautiful friend, was one of these Iraqis who were compelled to live with a false identity and a pseudonym. I did not know his real name until after his death, as was the case with most of the Iraqi strivers during that time.

Abd Al-Muhsin Barrak was one of the runaways from the Iraqi regime. Hepreferred to stay in Kuwait due to its closeness to his hometown in Az-Zubair district. He always dreamed that the regime would change one day so that he would be able to return to Iraq once more, but he did not know that his life would end in a land that wasas strange to him as he was to it.

Abu Barrak came to Kuwait atthe end of the seventies of the last century. He had a neurotic personality, he spoke fluent Arabic with a clear Iraqi accent, and he had a powerful voice. Abu Barrak suffered under the occupation more than we did, for he had to move from one place to another to hide from the Iraqi forces. He mostly came to us accompanied by the friend and writer Al-Rifa'y. When Abu Barrak came to visit, we would see the deep grief that occupied his soul and face – he, the one who'd escaped the bonfires of dictatorship and chosen Kuwait to be close to Iraq, and to Az-Zubair, his birthplace. The reason that forced him to leave Kuwaitwas simple: he found himself unable to bear the angry reactions of Kuwaitis when they heard his voice in markets and public places, or when he would mingle with them in general. They would distinguish his Iraqi accent anddisplay aggressiveness towards him.

Thus, he was compelled to travel to Bulgaria, and there he was diagnosed with cancer, perhaps due to hisdeep grief. His state of health pushed him to go to Jordan to be close to Iraq, and there he met with our common friend, Salah Hezayien. I still remember, bitterly and grievously, that phone call which came to me from Salah in 1993 while I was living in the UK to continue

my post-graduate studies, in which he consoled me for the death of
Abu Barrak, who'd passed away in a taxi on his way to the doctor.
When Salah asked me about the real name of Abu Barrak, he was
surprised that I really did not know it. I had to call our friend Ja'far
in Bulgaria, who was very close to him andwho eventually passed
away as well in Bulgaria, alone and expatriated, to enquire about
his name. Then I called Salah and gave him the real name of Abu
Barrak, and he did the burial procedures himself. I later knew that
Salah had covered the funeral expenses. There, Abu Barrak, that
Iraqi striver, passed away in a place that did not even know his
name.

The Egyptian director Farouk Abd Al-Aziz was also one of the
characters that astonished me. He was a friend and had a famous
weekly program in the Kuwaiti television. He never stopped
carrying his camera during the occupation, to record whatever
scenes, incidents, and faces that his eyes caught, to be a witness
of the daily happenings and atrocities of the invasion. I always
expected that he would combine that raw material that he captured
into an important documentary about the Iraqi invasion of Kuwait.
But after long years, I found out that he only presented a part of his
material in a collective film under the name of *Baraka,*[13] in which
he participated, but it did not find the fame or success that befitted
him and his effort, which never diminished during that difficult
time.

How can I forget that atmosphere that used to bring us
together with some prominent political figures – the atmosphere
of participating in lunches! The dearest person to my sister Nawal
was the parliament member and politician Abdullah Al-Naybari,
who would often share in our lunch while sitting on the floor with
us. Although Nawal did not always join us, the presence of that
parliament member in our house was enough to bring reassurance
to her.

---

[13] Arabic for blessing.

THE UNITED NATIONS

FTER SADDAM'S INVASION OF KUWAIT, we were greatly shocked and disappointed at the position of the Arab street[14] opposing Kuwait's liberation by the international coalition, which grew in some cases to support the invasion of Kuwait and even Saddam himself, particularly the positions of the religious movements, the Sunni[15] and the Shi'ite. On the other hand, there was a state of overwhelming anger among the Kuwaitis forthe betrayal and animosity expressed by these demonstrations that dominated the Arab street, especially by some nationalist and progressive movements, under the pretext of opposing the American presence in the region.

---

[14] The Arab street is an expression, in Arabic, referring to the spectrum of public opinion in the Arab world, often as opposed or contrasted to the opinions of Arab governments.

[15] This is not surprising. Afterwards, we discovered that even the religious movements of our country had the same position. The Kuwaiti ambassador in Washington during the Iraqi invasion, Sheikh Saud Nasser Al-Sabah, presented heavy criticism, in many interviews that were published by Kuwaiti and Arab newspapers, for some of the Kuwaiti Muslim Brotherhood figures when they requested meeting him as a civil delegation during the invasion in 1990. The meeting was to convince him of the inadmissibility of seeking the help of Americans to liberate Kuwait, and that the alternative was Islamic forces.

Sheikh Saud Nasser Al-Sabah: He was an ambassador of Kuwait in Washington during the invasion. He fought the battle inside the USA to obtain the Senate's approval for military intervention, until the painstaking efforts resulted in convincing the majority of the senate to vote for President Bush's decree for military intervention in Kuwait.

Within the Arab street, a certain faction displayed animosity towards us in a way that exceeded all others – the whole Jordanian street, with its crowds, parties, newspapers, and government that allsupported Saddam and opposed Kuwait. Naturally, nothing was comparable in animosity towards Kuwait except the Palestinian street in the occupied lands, for it witnessed massive demonstrations opposing the liberation of Kuwait and calling for the liberation of Palestine, demonstrations in which pictures of the executioner, Saddam Hussein, were raised that described him as the Liberator of Jerusalem.

In the midst of all this surreal vanity that we used to see and hear, Shaikha Al-Farhan called and told me that she waspreparing, with others, for a women's demonstration against the occupation in Al-Adiliya District, to be conducted at dusk of that day, and she informed me of the importance of rallying supportfor this demonstration. I told Nawal of the demonstration, and she displayed her desire to participate.

At the specified time, I drove my car, with Nawal, and passed by Shaikha on our way, then went to the assembly point in Damascus Street, which is the street separating Al-Rawdah and Al-Adiliya district. As soon as we left Al-Rawdah, we saw the congregation of women heading towards Al-Adiliya. A big SUV stopped in front of them, from which a young man got outand started handing over some posters tothe congregation.

I parked the car on the corner of the street, and we got off. The young man, Badr Al-Jai'an, whose identity I discoveredlater, handed us the said posters, and we saw that they carried the pictures of the Emir of Kuwait and his heir.

I greeted those who were present, most of whomwere known to us. The march began in a single line, by walking adjacent to Damascus Street. I saw my friend Iman Al-Baddah organizing the march's line. As for her sister, Amany, she held the loudspeaker and repeatedslogans rejecting and denouncing the occupation and stressing on the legitimacy under the rule of the Emir and his heir; the crowds were repeating these slogans after her.

When I sensed tiredness in Amany's voice, I took over the loudspeaker and started repeating the same passionate slogans. Throughout the demonstration, Amany and I were alternatelycarrying the loudspeaker and speaking. Badr Al-Jai'an and another assistant of his were recording a video of the demonstration.

We walked from the middle of Damascus road until we reached the Fourth Ring Road. Then we turned right and walked adjacent to the Fourth Circular. On the way, a truck carrying Iraqi soldiers passed by us. I felt fear at that moment, especially since a number of Iraqi soldiers had, two days earlier, had fired at a march that had taken place in Jabiriya District and in which the martyr Sana' Al-Foudary fell.

We continued our march towards the center of Al-Adiliya District, but when we reached the house at the beginning of the district, some women came out of their houses and askedus to go far away from their houses so that they could avoid being hit by the bullets of the occupation forces. Some of the area's residents displayed their solidarity with our march, but others were terrified of the tyrannical policy frequently followed by the Iraqi army against protestors or the resistance in general.

After a few days, a friend called me and told me that the video recorded during the march had beenrecorded by one of the Kuwaiti resistance members and that it had beensent to the Kuwaiti leadership in Saudi Arabia. It then had been played at a United Nations session in order to demonstrate the support of the Kuwaiti people who lived under the Saddamian occupation to the legitimate leadership of Kuwait under the rule of the Emir, Sheikh Jaber Al-Ahmad, and his heir, Saad Al-Abdullah Al-Sabah. He told me, at the same time, that the Iraqi forces hadphotos of the women who'd participated in that march and werelooking for them. As a result, he suggested that we had to take things easy and not leave the house for a while.

I grew afraid then, and I sat down to discuss the matter with my friends and family, especially since I was against not leaving the house. Among the friends with whom I discussed the matter was my neighbor Maha Al-Moqlad, who used to live in a part of the ground floor of the house. She had interests in beauty issues, for she owned a beauty salon at that time, and she had moved all its equipment to her house for fear of theft.

Maha suggested changing my outlook, and she challenged me by saying that she would make another Ekbal out of me. I accepted her challenge at once, and I went to her house, complying with all her instructions of cutting and dyeing my hair. She was assisted by the wife of my brother, Muhammad, whose brother Ali owned an eyeglasses shop. Therefore, she brought me two eyeglasses to use when I needed to go out.

I learned after the liberation from my sister Badriya, who had left us and goneto Muscat, that when Hanadi, Nawal's daughter, watched the march's pictures displayed in the Kuwaiti embassy in Oman, amongst which were pictures of her mother carrying a picture of the Emir, she'dbeenterrified. The pictures had been especially terrifying because ofthe spread of stories about the assault faced by Kuwaiti demonstrators fromthe occupation army, in addition to other stories about murders and rapes – among which were real stories, though others were mere exaggerations. However, they were sufficient for one idea to dominate Hanadi's mind: that her mother hadalso been killed in these demonstrations. This idea hadnot lefther mind until she'd received the first letter from her mother after that incident.

THE RED VEHICLE

A S SOON AS THE KUWAITI government left the country, it was replaced by a secret government concerned with managing the country's affairs. The collective public awareness of Kuwaitis in the country was a major factor in facilitating the affair management and the success of this government. For example, women did not need a governmental decree to wear black mantles, nor did the men need a decree to retain their beards, start civil disobedience, or stop going to work.

All these things happened in a completely spontaneous way and were adhered to by everyone, without exception. On the other end, several committees were formed to manage various affairs in the country, although the sources of these committees were different. For instance, some were distributing food supplies and securing the essential commodities; the cooperatives joined hands with solidarity committees to distribute supplies, very quickly, tomost Kuwaiti houses so that nearly all supply warehouses of the cooperatives were emptied to protect them from theft by occupation forces. The cooperatives were also keen to provide people, especially the military personnel thereof, with what they needed of raw materials and foods, and they delivered these materialsto their houses.

Due to my presence in Al-Rawdah, some of these committees contacted me to take account of the military personnel and the needy amongst people of the area. I noticed a concentration placed on the people of Block-1, known as the residents of Abdullah Al-Salim suburb, when Al-Rawdah District was not very large; it included a division of five blocks only, and Blocks 4 and 5 were separated by a main street called Al-Makhfar Street. Houses of the area became familiar to me, and I could count them one by one, especially after I had located, with Shaikha Al-Farhan, the vaults of the area and compiled a list of houses containing them as a precaution against the anticipated airstrike, as previously mentioned.

One day, a woman came to my house, introduced herself, and asked me, since I was a resident of the area, to help her take account of the number of military personnel in Block-1: to distribute supplies to them, to provide adequate houses for hiding, and to issue fake ID cards to facilitate their movement. I agreed to her request, and I informed Nawal of the task assigned to me and asked her to help me in the account-taking process. She immediately agreed.

We got in Sulaiman's small red car, which was parked in front of the house, and went around knocking on the district houses' doors and telling the residents the purpose of our visit. People of the district became familiar with me and Nawal, but for obvious security reasons, we did not reveal our full names. Two days later, after taking account of the houses where military personnel lived, we were surprised by Iraqi soldiers raiding a number of those houses looking for military personnel, and some of them were indeed arrested.

On the day following that disturbing Iraqi raid, one of the women living in Block-1, who knew us from our repeated visits tothem for one reason or another, came to our house. She told us that residents of Block-1 were searching for two sisters driving a small red car because they believed that they were the ones who'd provided the Iraqi soldiers with the information on the locations and addresses where Kuwaiti soldiers were hiding. She gave us the name of the person who'd adopted that suggestion and asked us to exercise care and caution.

Nawal and I did not leave the house that day. I called my aunt's husband, who lived in that block, and told him the story and what that woman told us.

Immediately, my aunt's husband went to visit that group, especially theman who sought revenge against us for his brother's arrest by the Iraqis. He told them what happened, saying, "The two sisters in the red car are only our daughters and have no connection whatsoever to that raid." Indeed, the uproar surrounding us started to calm down gradually. A few days later, I went on to resume my activities.

A STATE OF GRIEF

WE WERE INVITED BY OUR friend Laila Al-Qadi and her husband, Muhammad Borannan, to celebrate Christmas in a house where she was staying in the prestigious Al-Shuwaikh area, which was owned by one of the families that had left Kuwait. Laila had made more than one journey to Baghdad by bus as a part of the journeys organized by Kuwaitis, with the supervision of Dr. Ghanim Al-Najjar, to visit Kuwaiti captives and detainees in the Iraqi regime's detention centers.

Dr. Al-Najjar had played a prominent role in organizing these journeys during the occupation, the purpose of which was to organize visits for the families of detainees in a number of Iraqi governorates: Baqubah, Tikrit, Mosul, and Ramadi. Families were keen on conducting these journeys regularly, which undoubtedly contributed to raising the morale of the resilient in Kuwait and the captives in Iraq.

Every week, three buses at least would head to Iraq by land, loaded with people and with the families of captives and detainees. Dawwar Al-Izam square, near Sulaibikhat, became a launching point for buses. Families would head there, carrying what they could of money, food, and cigarettes, enduring risks and difficulties as well as the harassment of the Iraqi intelligence, particularly after the number of contributors in organizing these journeys increased, the growth in part due to the enthusiasm and support of the country's youth for them.

I remember that I called Dr. Al-Najjar one day to register for my cousin Ibtisam. She was a recently married young woman who'd lost both her husband and her father, for they had been members of the Kuwaiti Armed Forces and had been taken captive.

In the early morning, I accompanied Ibtisam to the bus assembly point. After I had parked my car on the side of the road, Ibtisam got off, carrying her luggage towards the bus. Dr. Al-Najjar came to greet me with his usual smile, so we stood chatting. Meanwhile, I heard a scream from Dr. Ghanim, and before I understood what was happening, I found him pushing me strongly towards the car; he then bent over and stuck himself to the car alongside me, and I caught sight of a huge truck, on board which werea number of Iraqi soldiers, moving towards us at a very high speed, nearly running us over. Had it not been for the quick reactions of Dr. Ghanim, and perhaps divine providence, both of us would have been among the dead.

Laila Al-Qadi had just come back from Iraq from what would turn out to be herlast journey to Iraq; it had preceded by a few days the coalition's airstrike to liberate Kuwait. Coincidentally, as she told us, she had met on her way back a young man who looked sad; his name was Kifaa. When Laila spoke to him, she realized that this young man was sad because of his yearning forhis parents and the atmosphere of Christmas, which he used to celebrate every year with his mother, Vera, and his father, Sadeq. Motivated by maternal instincts, Laila decided to celebrate Christmas to fulfill Kifaa's desire and invited a number of foreigners who used to live, hidden, in the homes of some Kuwaitis.

The celebration gained a special importance, especially because it took place shortly before the airstrike on Iraq, before Desert Storm – Kuwait's liberation operation. In that operation, 34 states participated and formed a coalition the likes of which hasrarely been seen in history, led by the United States of America. The mere thought of that huge military buildup to liberate Kuwait was frightening for us; it instilled in us a sense of an ambiguous destiny. The way war was to be initiated, and what would arise from it, was strange and a source of panic and fear. It never left our minds – the weapons of mass destruction, including chemical and biological weapons that might be used in this war, particularly with the possibility that the Kuwaiti grounds would be a battlefield for these lethal weapons. The idea of war, which we had neither experienced nor witnessed before, was a source of great anxiety and fear. Whenever I expressed my fears regarding that, my sister's husband Baba-Oud would reassure me and say, "The protector is God. What is the worst thing that could happen?" Then he would add, to drive away any mysterious ghoststhatsurrounded us, "We are the ones who chose to remain in the midst of everything. Therefore, we must accept the consequences of our choice." It wastrue that we were the ones to choose, but thinking about war brings about the strange and unknown!

On Christmas Day's morning, I tried to keep my composure and act calmly; I drove the ghost of war away from my mind and drove my car, heading for Qurtuba District, where my friend Haya lived. As I arrived at her house, I found that she had prepared the raisin-stuffed Christmas cake – the British way. From her house, we headed together to the house of Laila Al-Qadi in Al-Shuwaikh area, which seemed deserted to us, as if it were aghost town; many of its inhabitants had left the country during the invasion.

When we arrived at the house, I parked my car out front. We passed the house's garden and went to the kitchen, whichlooked spacious. There, Laila greeted us with a smile and cheerfulness. Then she led us to take a look atthe preparations she had made for the party, and we greeted her husband, Muhammad Al-Jaza'iry, who was of Algerian Nationality. He looked occupied with preparing food. Under the stairs, the children's gifts were placed, which were notebooks and pens brought by Kifaah, in whose honor the party was organized. I learned that he'd brought them from the school owned by his father in partnership with his mother. Laila's brother, Khalid, acted the role of Santa Clause, wearing his outfit that had beenbrought by a friend from Sultan Center grocery store. Najat As-Sultan (may God have mercy on her soul) decorated the dining table with leaves, spread some sand over the table, and garnished it with some Kuwaiti coins that had lost their value after dealings in them were abolished by decree of the Iraqi tyrant. Multi-colored fruit were arranged in a way that represented the Kuwaiti flag. The number of attendees was large, and I did not know many of them, but I recognized some of the attendees, including the late Fahd Al-Shayei' and his wife, Hamid Al-Hammoud, Dr. Yusuf Al-Ibrahim and his wife, Khalid Al-Qadi and his wife, Ziyad Al-Da'eij, Alaa' Al-Ateeqi, and others, in addition to the presence of a number of foreigners of both genders.

Prior to the approach of the curfew hours, the number of people arriving increased, which made us worry, particularly since we knew that the curfew started after 5 pm and that there was a threat of shooting at anyone who violated the curfew, whether by walking or driving. Perhaps the surprise was when Laila told us that her husband had obtained a license to organize the party from the soldiers guarding Al-Shuwaikh area. The cars of the invitees were lined up in front of the house, the husband was careful to bribe the soldiers using money, and he sent them meals of food as well, and so they welcomed him and his guests.

This Christmas celebration managed to draw smiles on children's faces, maybe even on the faces of the adult men and women, and it spread a state of happiness and joy in the hearts of everybody. The invitees scattered about in the halls of the house that were open to each other, in the kitchen, the library, and the garden. What gathered them was conversation about the upcoming war, which was scheduled to start on the fifteenth of January, 1991. This date was the final deadline given by the Security Council for the withdrawal of the Iraqi forces from Kuwait. However, nobody knew how things would turn out. There was a lot of anxiety, fear, and panic, but at the same time, there was an overwhelming desire for life that was expressed in enjoying that party. Time passed without any of the attendees paying attention to the curfew.

The party represented moments of simple happiness, which we stole away from grief and anger, where thoughts, feelings, and emotions were mixed. There, I found myself leaving Al-Shuwaikh with my friend Haya near midnight.

VOLUNTARY WORKS

URING THE OCCUPATION, I WORKED with many organizations. I used to receive several calls from these organizations seeking my aid in delivering a certain piece of information or item to someone, especially the residents of Al-Rawdah. Sometimes, I would receive calls from people who deliberately hid their real identities or the real purpose of their request to protect the secrecy of the organization or entity that they belong to in reality.

What I remember in that regard were a number of women who contacted me to provide the needy with wheat and rice, and sometimes with money.

These grants were not frequent or regular, but theyprovided support for many of the needy, at least in fulfilling some momentary urgent needs.

I remember that one of the women who used to contact me was Ms. Manal Badr, who called me and asked me to attend meetings of the association that was founded then and called "Women and Children of Kuwait's Association." I assumed the role of the association's rapporteur throughout the invasion, and I undertook recording down all the meeting proceedings of the association with my handwriting.

After the liberation, Sheikh Saad Al-Abdullah requested to meet the association's board, so Ms. Manal invited the board members for a meeting that preceded our appointment with him, and we all agreed that in order for our meeting to be fruitful, we must organize ourselves. This organization necessitated that we distribute the questions that had crossed our minds and that we wished to have answered by Sheikh Saad Al-Abdullah with complete honesty and transparency.

We distributed the important questions among us, making sure that each of us adhered to one specified question to His Highness so that we could cover all the aspects that we wished to cover in that meeting.

I distributed the questions, written, tothe board members, and we went to the Amiri Diwan (Diwan of the Prince)[16] in Al-Shamiya suburb, which was initially used by Sheikh Saad Al-Abdullah as headquarters to assume his functions. As soon as I entered, I found many people in the Diwan, among whom was Dr. Ahmad Al-Rubei, who had just gotten out of the office of His Highness.

The secretary called for us to enter the meeting room and meetthe Sheikh, who stood up to greet each one of us and then asked us to sit around a large table, which I think had used to be the Diwan dining table.

The Sheikh began his speech by praising God on the passing of the crisis and that Kuwait, as well as we, had gotten out of it in one piece. Then he enquired about us. The president of association handed himthe handwritten meeting proceedings and explained what we had done. After asking one or two of the previously prepared questions, the conversation started going in a different direction than what had been planned, and there was no hope for the conversation to return to the agreed-upon arrangement. I went out after the end of the meeting feeling what the famous phrase means: "It is as if you never fought, O Bozaid!"

There was also another group that included many of my friends where we would meet periodically. We would go to these meetings in my car, so I would begin by picking up my friend Shaikha Al-Farhan, then we would go to Hanaa' Al-Mnayis' house, and afterwards to the dear Amal Al-Ghanim, for we almost lived on the same block. Then we would head to our almost-monthly meeting, where we would exchange news, whether about our families inside or abroad, and then we would provide ourselves with our stock

---

16 DiwanAl-Babtain in Al-Shamiya Suburb.

of the "NationalResistance Bulletin," which used to be issued by the "Kuwaiti Resistance Movement" (HAMAK) during the Iraqi invasion, in order to distribute it tothe people.

The purpose of this bulletin was to support those who wereresilient inside the country, boost their morale, and provide them with information to cope with the Saddamian Ba'athist media in the country. I remember once that Shaikha Al-Farhan asked me to deliver a number of issues of that bulletin to Sheikh Al-Basir,[17] may God have mercy on his soul, in his house in Al-Adiliya. I picked up Shaikha, and when we arrived, he welcomed us into his Diwan. Since he was blind, may God have mercy on his soul, I did not feel embarrassed to put my hand in my dress to grab the issues, hand them to him, and exchange them for the poem he had written during that time and wished to publish in the bulletin. Until now, his voice still rings in my ears, and his words still whisper to us, "Take care of yourselves and look out, girls." We greeted him and then bid farewell while he waved his hand, praying for safety and protection for us.

---

[17] The author Abd Al-Razik Al-Basir (1919-1999) was the librarian of Publications & Press Department library in 1956, the librarian of the Ministry of Information's library until 1991, a member of the Media Advisory Board, a member of the National Council for Culture, Art & Literature, a member of the Arab Heritage, Research & Translation Committee, a member of the National Cultural Club in 1952, a member of the Writers Association, and a member of the Academy of the Arabic Language in Cairo; he was nominated for this position by Dr. Taha Hussein and held it until his death.

MARRIAGE

O NE EARLY MORNING, AFTER NEARLY two months of the occupation, Azza, my Egyptian friend, called me. "Ekbal, how are you?"

I answered, bombarding her with questions, "Who? Azza? I can't believe it. You didn't travel? Are you still in Kuwait? What are you doing here?"

Azza responded, "I will tell you everything, but I must see you. I need your help with something."

I askedher, "What is it Azza?"

"I met an Egyptian man. I got to know him when I requested his help to move my belongings in preparation for travel, and a romantic relationship quickly grew between us, but it was real. He does not wish for our relationship to be an illicit one, so he asked to marry me, and now we are searching for a marriage officiant to officiate our marriage."

I replied, overjoyed, "It is nice to hear that someone seeks happiness amidst all the tyranny and destruction that we are living here in Kuwait."

"Ekbal, we need a man of religion to officiate the marriage."

I replied, "Ok, Azza, I will ask around and get back to you."

"Ekbal, we want to get married today."

I then remembered a verse from a poem by the Iraqi poet friend, exiled in London, Abd Al-Karim Qasid, as he recalled his childhood in his Diwan,[18]"Knocking on childhood's doors":*Do people still get married in these times?*

---

[18] Diwan has multiple meanings in Arabic; it could mean a collection of poems by the same author, a high government body, or a bureau.

I replied, "Ok, Azza, I will get back to you shortly."

I hung up the phone, filled with joy and thinking, "Why not? Let's rejoice a little."

I went to my sister's husband, Muhammad, to ask him about it. He said that he would ask the mosque's imam when he wentto pray the Noon Prayer whether he could officiate the marriage.

The imam agreed, so I called Azza, and she came with the husband-to-be and two friends as witnesses. We sat in the hall waiting for the arrival of Muhammad and theimam after Sunset Prayer to officiate the marriage.

My sister's husband came back alone, so we asked him, "Where is the mosque's imam?" He answered, "The imam believed that the spouses-to-be are Kuwaitis, but when I told him they were Egyptians, he refused because he did not know what the procedures would be afterwards. He facilitates the affairs of Kuwaitis until the official government returns to certify the marriage contracts, but he does not know anything about the affairs of other foreign communities."

I felt disappointed for failing to fulfill the hopes of these two lovers to become spouses. Then Saad, who'd come as a witness, was a fifty-year-old man, a poet, and who worked in a publication house, suggested, "I have the solution."

I said to him, "What is the solution?"

He said, "I will make their marriage official right now."

I asked him, "How?"

He said, "Give me a notebook and a pen."

Saad sat on the ground after pushing the table aside, and started writing. He had beautiful writing that I had never seen the likes of before, as if he werean Arab-calligraphy artist. He started repeating what he waswriting aloud so that he looked, indeed, as if he werea preacher in a Hussainiya.

The whole thing was unfamiliar to me, especially since this was my first time attending a wedding ceremony.

Saad asked Azza and Moustafa to sit on the floor beside him. Then he began writing and saying what he wrote aloud:

On this day, a customary marriage is written, with the express acceptance and agreement between:

1- *Mr. Moustafa, residing in Kuwait, whose nationality is Egyptian and whose religion is Islam,*
2- *Ms. Azza residing in Kuwait, whose nationality is Egyptian and whose religion is Islam,*

Both parties have certified to their capacity to contract and dispose, their freedom of any legal barrier. They have agreed that the First Party (Moustafa) acknowledges, before the witnesses stated in this contract, after express acceptance and agreement, that he has accepted marriage to the Second Party (Azza), a legal marriage according to the Book of God, and the Sunnah (way) of his Messenger, peace be upon him, and in compliance with the provisions of Islamic Sharia.

Both parties agree on a dowry of ten Kuwaiti dinars, paid by the First Party, at the contract location, to the hand of the Second Party.

The Second Party also acknowledges, after express acceptance and agreement, that she has accepted marriage to the First Party, a legal marriage according to the Book of God, and the Sunnah (way) of his Messenger, peace be upon him, and in compliance with the provisions of Islamic Sharia.

Lastly, both parties accept all the provisions of this contract, as required by the provisions of Islamic Sharia, and the legal implications that may result from it, particularly filiation; their children from this marriage have all the legal rights before them.

He made two copies of the contract, both handwritten; one copy was given to Azza and the other to Moustafa after they'd been by them as well as the witnesses.

The attendees wished the spouses a happy marriage. I went to kiss Azza and congratulate Saad, and I attempted to ululate, although I did not have that traditional skill that many women master.

The wedding was performed, and the spouses left our house to their new happy house.

A week later, she called me to say goodbye, for they had decided to return to Egypt.

Sadly, I heard and learned afterwards that their marriage did not last more than one month after returning to Egypt, after which they were divorced.

UNCLE, UNCLE

BEFORE THE COALITION AND US forces started the airstrike, my brother Muhammad came to our house in Al-Rawdah with his wife, Fadila, and their two sons, Fahd, who was two years old, andthe elder Nassir, who was almost three years of age. Muhammad and his family lived in the Sulaibikhat area that lies in the northern part of Kuwait, near the Iraqi borders. Their house is situated near the sea, and it has a large garden.

Due to the house being located close to the sea, in addition to being situated close to the Northern Road that leads to Iraq, some of the Iraqi soldiers thought it was necessary for the residents to evacuate the house.

However, Fadila, Muhammad's wife, refused. Yet instead of causing problems, she managed, with her gentle and logical way, to convince the soldiers of their inability to leave the house – she and her husband and children. She clarified to them, "Leaving the house means becoming homeless on the streets with the children." Indeed, the Iraqi officer who was the leader of the group assigned to evacuate the house changed his mind and found it sufficient to seize control of the house's garden; Fadila agreed to that compromise.

I asked Muhammad, saying, "How did you sleep with soldiers in your garden?"

Without thinking much, he replied, "They never bothered us." Then he added, "Can you imagine that they installed an anti-aircraft cannon in the garden?"

Then he added sarcastically, "Can you believe that Fahd and Nassir were able to befriend the soldiers, so much so that they became agents for the Iraqi soldiers?"

Then my brother, Muhammad, smiled and started to tell me of the state of the soldiers with a hint of sarcasm: "Nassir and Fahd were happy with the cannon installed in the garden. Whenever they heard or saw a plane in the sky, they went to the officer in charge and told him, 'Uncle, Uncle, a plane... a plane.' Then the officer directed the anti-aircraft cannon in the direction where theypointed and started to fire."

With some panic, I told him, "Muhammad, watch out for them, God bless you, or stray bullets might hit them."

He calmly tried to reassure me, and clarified, "It is ok... they are playing and happy with this anti-aircraft game."

I turned to Fadila, enquiring, "And you, how do you deal with them?"

She replied, "They are nice. They do not go past the garden unless they need tea or water."

AL-TARAB DISTRICT

ALAH HEZAYIEN HAD TO TRAVEL to Jordan. Before he left, I asked
Nawal, Baba-Oud, and the kids to record a tape to send to
Muscat, and I told them that Salah was the one who would
deliver it to my sister Badriya and her family where they had settled. I
suggested that we record the tape after finishing the house chores, and
I also suggested, for security reasons, that the tape be cheerful, light,
without crying, and without referring to the Iraqi occupation forces.

At about 11 am on theday that we agreed to record the tape, we
gathered around the dining table, prepared the recorder, and began
speaking to it in order to record our voices, to send our regards to
Badriya, her husband, Talib, and their children. After greetings, we gave
a detailed presentation of our daily life and referred to people who used
to visit us during these difficult times. Then Nawal took the recorder
and started giving advice to Hanadi, her daughter, encouraging her to
look after her brother Khalaf, may God have mercy on his soul, who
died after returning to Kuwait in a car accident.

After we were done recording all what we wished to say and
record, I decided to send them something cipher-like, to explain to
them, in a nearly sarcastic way, what was going on in the country.
I started to ask questions ofAisha, Sarah, and all who were there
about the new names for the Kuwaiti districts that had beenchosen
by the Iraqi occupation forces. I felt as I was asking these questions
as if I werein a children's TV show. I began with Abdullah Al-Salim
District and said, "What is its name?"

So Aisha answered loudly, "Basra District."

We all laughed at her enthusiastic quick response, and then her
mother told me in astonishment, "Yes… yesterday when we went
to the suburb's complex, I saw the name written on the signboard."

Then I asked them another question, "Very good, Aisha. What about Jabiriya?"

Then everybody repeated loudly in a laughing voice, "Al-Nidaa' District."

Whenever I asked one of the children to accompany me to my house in Jabiriya to get some stuff, Nawal would always ask me where I was headed, and I would answer, "Going to Al-Nidaa' District." Then, Kuwaiti districts started having new names:

Al-Salmiya: Al-Nasr District

Al-Shuwaikh: Al-Rashid District.

Salwa: Al-Khansa' District

Sabah Al-Salim: Al-Thawra (Revolution) District. "I do not know what revolution the residents of Sabah Al-Salim had."

All throughout the game, I was trying to find the names of the areas that had been named after one of the Kuwaiti rulingfamily members, which hadbeen changed by the Iraqi regime. When we finished saying the names of some districts that I had not passed by during that time, I asked the audience my final question about the new name of Al-Rawdah District, and none of them answered. So I repeated the question again, approached the recorder with my mouth, and said, "Don't you know that name of Al-Rawdah District?"

And without waiting for an answer, I said, "Al-Tarab District."[19] Nawal, Muhammad and I burst into laughter, while the children remained silent, for they did not know the meaning of what I had said. I remember that after Kuwait's liberation, we went to visit my sister Badriya, who lived in Muscat, and after she prepared my favorite "Green" tea, we sat drinking the tea in her garden. After talking about the conditions of the country and telling the stories, Badriya whispered in my ear, "Ekbal, God bless you, why did they, God curse them, name Al-Rawdah after Al-Tarab District?"

---

[19] Al-Tarab District: An unofficial whorehouse in Basra, inhabited by a group of gypsies. It is the second whorehouse in Basra after Bashar Street that was established by the Iraqi government then to limit the prostitution phenomenon. The district consists of a number of mud houses inhabited by gypsies and their clients.

THE SISTER

THE WAIT WAS DIFFICULT, PARTICULARLY since what I waswaiting for could be mydoom, but I was impatiently anticipating it nonetheless. Wasit "waiting for Godot," waiting for something that would never come? It had all become pointless, futile. I had to put a stop to the futility I wasliving, but how?

On a winter day in January, I woke up from my usual nap, and I switched through radio stations, looking for good news, but all stations were busy with news of the New Year. I did not hear any news about our issue, as if we'd been pushed aside in order not to spoil the New Year celebrations.

Despite the fact that Christmas and New Year celebrations usually spread joy and fill people with happiness you can see in their faces, theyalways made me feel lonely. That feeling had become associated with me during my expatriation and years of study all over the planet, since Christmas celebrations usually have a familial character. Friends leave the campus and return to their families to celebrate at their homes, whilewe foreign students usually remain alone in the almostempty dormitories or the campus.

The weather was getting colder, and the sky was cloudy. I went to the hall and found Baba-Oud and my uncle Abd Al-Razik, may God have mercy on their souls, sittingwith my brother Sulaiman, drinking tea and smoking their cigarettes. I dragged myself and sat down with them.

Baba-Oud asked me, "So, what is new?"

I briefly replied, "Nothing."

The news of killing and barbarity reaching me had increased, which had heightened the state of despair and boredom that had gotten to me recently, especially after hearing the previous day the story of the martyr, Mubarak Al-Nout, that brave unionist who'd worked during the invasion as a director of Al-Ardiya complex. He'd supervised the complex's organization and distribution of food supplies tocitizens. He had refused the entrance of Iraqi soldiers to the complex, and he'd refused to deal in the Iraqi Dinar. In one of their provocative visits, the Iraqi intelligence officers had told him to bring down the Emir's portrait from the wall and hang Saddam's portrait instead. When he'd refused, they'd dragged him to the courtyard of the complex, gotten the citizens out, and shot him in the head while he was blindfolded.

While I was absentminded, lost in my silent world…

I heard my uncle's laugh as he said, "Today, the glass is shut."[20]

I replied, "I am tired of living like this."

Then I heard yelling of children in the next room.

I went on, "Enough. I don't want to hear kids' voices. I am tired of it."

My uncle remained silent, but Sulaiman laughed. He saidto Baba-Oud, "What say we put the kids in bags and take them to the school to the Iraqi soldiers and say that Ekbal got tired of them?"

Everybody laughed, but I did not find it funny.

In the evening, I got a call from our friend Salah Hezayien, inviting me to meet him in his house in Hawalli District. He had decided to leave the next day, and a number of friends had gathered at his house to bid him farewell. I went quickly to Nawal to take the letters and recorded tapes that she wanted to send to her children in Muscat, and I told her that Salah would betravelling the next morning.

I hurried to my brother Sulaiman and asked him to drive me to Hawalli to say goodbye to Salah and give him the letters heading to Muscat. Sulaiman looked at his watch and replied, "Oh, kind one,

---

[20] It means that the person does not want to talk, so he has shut the glass of his window.

it is now 8 o'clock, and Hawalli is a problematic area that should not be visited at night. Let us go early in the morning."

However, I insisted on going and convinced him that it was only for an hour, that we would take my uncle with us, and that nothing would happen to us, especially because he carried the certificate (of non-interference signed by Hassan Al-Majid).

I put on my mantle, took the tapes and messages, hid them in my clothes as a precaution, and we left.

As soon as our car turned towards Tunisia Street in Hawalli District, we saw a battalion of the Republican Guard (the Red Berets) blocking the road and searching cars entering the district.

Here, fear overcame us, and Sulaiman started to blame me. "Didn't I tell you that this area is not safe? And to make things worse, these are not regular army, but Republican Guard."

I remained silent for a short while, and then I answered, "No, it will be alright, God willing. You just give them the certificate, and they will let you go."

I was appalled by the scene of people who were stopped for reasons unknown to me.

It came to our turn, so Sulaiman opened the car window, and one of them asked him, "Identity."

Here, Sulaiman gave him his civil ID, and the guard asked Sulaiman, "Where do you work?"

I then asked Sulaiman to give him the certificate that it might alleviate his flood of questions.

Sulaiman gave him the certificate, and as soon as the guard read it, he said, "Stay here," and went to his superior. Sulaiman looked at me in a blaming fashion once more. "I didn't want to give it to him. See, now it's become a big matter. He went to his superior."

I did not understand, but I saw the officer in charge and two guards come towards us. They asked Sulaiman to get off the car. Here, the officer looked inside the car and said to Sulaiman, "Who is with you in the car?"

Sulaiman answered, "My sister and my uncle."

The man looked at my uncle, who was sitting in the back, and said, "Take her" – pointing at me – "and go home." He then looked at Sulaimanand said, "You come with us."

Sulaiman asked him for the reason, and the officertold him that the license he wascarrying wasfake.

Once I heard this, before they could take him, I opened the car door and hurried towards them, screaming, "Why are you taking him? Who told you that the certificate is a fake? Call Hassan Al-Majid and ask him about my brother Sulaiman. If he said that he does not know him, then take him, but I won't leave until you call Hassan Al-Majid, and right now!" I was in complete hysteria, so much so that I did not know what I was saying.

The officer moved away a little and spokewith the other. Shortly, he came back and saidto my brother Sulaiman,"We are returning you because of your sister. Nowgo."

As soon as Sulaiman got in the car and we were heading towards Salah's house, he said to me, "You are always getting me into trouble."

I told him, "How am I getting you into trouble. Had it not been for me, you would not have come back. Didn't he tell you 'Go back because of your sister'?"

Sulaiman answered, laughing, "No, they said 'Go back, because your sister is crazy.' If anybody else had said what you said, the Republican Guard would have had the right to take him. I swear to God, when I heard you, my heart sank." He laughed, and my uncle laughed with him.

To this day, I still ask myself, "How on earth did I say what I said?"

ISMAIL FAHD ISMAIL[21]

WE WERE STILL SUFFERING FROM scarcity of water and food in Kuwait as a result of the severe shortage of food, especially bread. During the last few months of the invasion, we had baked the (Indian Chapati) bread; it had only required us to prepare a dough of flour and water, spread the dough, and then put it in a pan, cooking it until its side becamered and then turning it onto the other side.

On the second morning of Kuwait's liberation (Kuwait was liberated on February 26, 1991), I stood in the kitchen preparing Chapati when my neighbor Maha came and asked me to go with her to visit a common friend who lived in Bayan District and get some bread from their house, since we knew that their living conditions mightbe better than ours. Once we arrived at Ismail's house in Bayan District, I was surprised by the emergence of Sheikh Ali Al-Salim,[22] masked, from their house. I greeted him, since we worked in the same organization. He greeted me back and disappeared.

I went into the house, and our friend's husband, our novelist friend, Ismail Al-Fahd, welcomed us with his usual smile, greeted us, and asked us to sit and have tea; my dear friend Laila

---

[21] Ismail Fahd Ismail: A Kuwaiti novelist, born in 1940. He is considered the real founder of the art of the novel in Kuwait. His first novel, *The Sky is Blue*, which uncovered his excellent talent, was introduced by the renowned Egyptian author, Salah Abd El-Sabour, in 1970, who said about it, "I find that this is the novel of the century." Ismail has written around forty novels and stories.

[22] Ali Salim Al-Ali Al-Sabbah, born in 1950, was a former Minister of Finance and of Transportation.

Al-Othman was also there in the hall. I noticed in the other assembly the presence of Sheikh Ahmad Al-Fahd[23] and others; they looked like they had just finished a meeting.

Ismail enquired about me, and we chatted about the invasion, which we all agreed was like a nightmare. A conversation started between Ismail and me about the armed resistance, particularly since I knew he was one of the leaders of the "Abu Al-Fuhoud Group"[24] in the Kuwaiti Resistance.

I asked him, "Ismail, I know that the resistance movement started spontaneously and automatically in all districts. Kaifan's District kept fighting and remained surrounded for a while, and some battles took place around it, similarly for Rumaithiya District, but it stopped after a while. However, your group kept going in Al-Rawdah"– where his father's house was –"and we residents of Al-Rawdah suffered a lot due to the acts of armed resistance and your killing of the soldiers in the police office, which resulted in the retributory reaction of Iraqi soldiers, who oppressed, choked, and harassed us."

I continued, "The Kuwaiti forces, which resisted the Iraqi invasion and fought many battles against the invading forces, were not able to endure because it was an unequal battle, one which ended in the occupation of Kuwait. So, what about us, when we are unarmed people? I think that we ought to have known our capabilities and powers before raising arms against them. Was civil disobedience not sufficient as a means of resistance?"

---

[23] Sheikh Ahmad Al-Fahd, born in 1960, is that eldest son for Sheikh Fahd Al-Ahmad Al-Sabbah, who died as a martyr on August 2, 1990, at the hands of the Iraqi Army upon the Iraqi invasion of Kuwait, at the gates of Dasman Palace. He was called 'Dasman's Martyr'.

[24] The group was called "Abu Al-Fuhoud Group" in honor of the martyr Fahd Al-Ahmad, who was assassinated on the first day of the barbaric invasion, when he went to repel the attack on Dasman Palace. The group led by Ahmad Al-Fahd had performed operations against the Iraqi Army, the most famous of which was shooting down the civilian plane in Farwaniya governorate. As for Ali Salim Al-Ali, he was the one responsible for financing and delivering money into Kuwait during the invasion.

Ismail was displeased at what I had said, and told me that my opinion was wrong. Heasked, "How, then, will we show our rejection of the occupation?" Then he added sharply, "Sacrifices have to be made."

I saw grief and anger strike his face, and he tried hard to hide it. I learned later that this was only due to his belief in what he and his group had done, which included his young brother Badr, the judge, who'd been captured during a resistance operation and executed by Iraqi soldiers.

I was, and still am, of the position that violence will not solve any problem. Rather, the solution must bebasedon responsible dialogue or peaceful resistance, like the one planted by Gandhi in his resistance to the British occupation. I strongly believe that Gandhi's policy (Satyagraha) is the force that produces truth and love, or nonviolence, and that the "eye for an eye" principle will result in an entirely blind world.

One of the means of civil resistance is civil disobedience, which Kuwaitis implemented throughout the invasion, and which aims to defeat the other with its positive impacts. Perhaps my position to renounce weapons, military solutions, and violence originated from having lived a long period of my life in India. That Indian society, which constitutes around one sixth of the earth's population, with its racial, religious, and sectarian diversity, forced the British Empire to leave India using the culture of tolerance and nonviolence adopted by that nation. That is why I notice the effects of the culture of that nation –a nation that is peaceful and a strong believer in peaceful resistance, tolerance, and nonviolence – on me.

I also admit that the nonviolent culture is a humane one, and although it is not a complete culture – since it does not possess the complete truth – the global experience has proven the defectiveness of generalizing a certain approach toall cases. Adopting a resistance approach may be suitable to the nature of the people or the entire objective situation; every case is unique, and a successful experience imposes its ideology upon others.

LIBERATION

O N JANUARY 17, 1991, KUWAIT's liberation operation, a.k.a. Operation Desert Storm, began. The coalition's air force struck the Iraqi military sites while we anticipated, in panic, news of the war through the radio, and at the same time awaited the favorable signs of liberation. Waiting and anticipating how things would turn out exhausted us. Over time, the occupation soldiers' aggressiveness towards us increased, and their oppression and vengeance intensified. They arrested civil young and grown men from in front of their houses, from the streets, and from mosques, and these men were deported to Basra. They also attacked Al-Qurain's house,[25] which housed a number of resistance members. The house was destroyed, and 12 members of the resistance who were there at that time were killed after a fierce battle between the two sides. Great stress befell them; was it the smashing sound of the storm that I had seen in my dream, which had tried to uproot my father's *Nabk* tree? Or was it the bells of salvation?

February 25 passed very heavily, particularly since it happened to be the 30th anniversary of Kuwait's independence. Great tiredness came upon us that night, and we felt that exhaustion completely overtook us; we knew not how we spent that night or the means by which we slept. However, what astonished us was the calmness that

---

[25] Al-Qurain's house: A house in Al-Qurain suburb that was a center for Kuwaiti resistance (Al-MassilaGroup). A battle took place there on February 24, 1991, between members of the Iraqi Army and 12 members of the Kuwaiti resistance, who were all killed in that battle. The National Council for Culture, Art & Literature turned the house into a mosque to commemorate the martyrs' memory.

dominated the next morning. It was a calm that indicated fear, or perhaps it was the calm before the storm.

When I woke up and sat up in my bed, I noticed that Sulaiman was leaving the house. I got up, sneaking calmly to follow his steps; I noticed Sarah following her uncle. Calmly, we saw him sneaking towards the roof. As I watched him with Sarah, we saw him open the door leading to the roof's courtyard to see what was happening outside. Before he got out, I yelled at him, afraid that a stray bullet might hit him. He ignored my warning and headed to the roof's fence; he kept his head down to avoid being seen by anyone. Once he'd taken position at the fence, he heard a voice coming from a neighbor's house thatdeclared the disappearance of soldiers and officers from the street. Although I had heard the same voice, I was still afraid of stray bullets and feared this silence might be followed by another round of airstrikes from the coalition forces.

However, I took my courage and headed to the roof's courtyard. Once there, I found the roofs of our neighbors' houses were filled with people like us, wondering about the secret of this scary silence.

There, we saw helicopters flying in our sky, and I thought to myself, "Oh my God! What is happening?" Then we realized they were the coalition's helicopters. Since they were flying close to us, the crew saluted us, and as soon as we saw their hands waving, all women ululated in happiness. Then Sarah hurried to her parents to deliver news of the great happening. The signs of relief and pleasure manifested on the faces of everybody. While I was watching the happy scene, I saw a group of young men reach the site near our house and start to remove the dust off the hole they had dug on the first day of the Iraqi occupation. They dug out the weapons they had hidden and started happily waving them and dancing.

Once Nawal reached the roof with her husband, I showered her with hugs and kisses, and our eyes flooded with happy tears. While we were in this state, Aisha came to tell me that the girl we were hosting from the orphanage refused to come to the roof and wouldnot stop crying by the stairs. I hurried towards her and found that she was crying nonstop.

Surprised at her state, I asked her, "Dear, what is wrong?"

Ekbal Al-Othaimeen

She continued crying and ignored my question. I cried with her and started petting her hair while trying to tempt her to come and watch the planes with me. She surprised me by saying, in a clear bitterness, "I don't want to go, because I know you will return me to the orphanage today."

Mother Hayfaa' said, "When the liberation happens, you will come back." I tried to reassure her by saying, "I will not return you now. We will all celebrate the liberation, and you will stay with us longer." She smiled in delight, so I kissed her and accompanied her to the roof's courtyard to celebrate with the neighbors.

After half an hour of being on the roof, we went down, exhausted, and found ourselves wondering what to do. The children wanted to go out to celebrate, and I asked them to clean the house first, shower, and then go celebrate. My sister Nawal agreed with me. The children calmed down, and I found them hurrying to organize the house and distributing the work between them. Nawal took over the kitchen, I decided to wash the courtyard and garden, and the rest were distributed on the houserooms. I do not know why I delayed the celebration. Was it because I could not bear happiness in a single dose? Or perhaps I feared the surge of emotions. No matter; I held the mop and started to wash the courtyard. When I was done, I opened the front door and started washing the street in front of the house.

I did not see any sign of life in the streets. It was like a place struck by a volcano. Perhaps this was one of the most famous volcanoes in the history of the country, for this volcano was accompanied by fissures, sounds, and earthquakes that struck at the root of this country for a period seven months. But, over time, volcanoes cool down and get buried under the ashes, although the ashes remain hot. There was a layer of volcanic ash thatI wastrying to remove! Was I washing the street or washing that era? In that moment, my friendHaya arrived, and when she got out of her car, we started hugging and crying. She was going to celebrate in the Flag Square; I told her that I wasgoing to follow her to the celebration. I had longed for happiness, and my passion had increased even more from the blood flowing with the love of this country. However, I preferred to remain quiet, for the blood had escaped my heart, and only the ashes remained.

Ekbal Al-Othaimeen

Printed in the United States
By Bookmasters